JUNIOR MAGIC SERMON-TALKS

JUNIOR MAGIC SERMON-TALKS

By
JACOB J. SESSLER
*Author of "Communal Pietism Among Early
American Moravians," "Christianity
Marches On," and "Saints and
Tomahawks"*

NEW YORK
Fleming H. Revell Company
LONDON AND EDINBURGH

Printed in the United States of America

New York: 158 Fifth Avenue
London: 21 Paternoster Square

PREFACE

OLD and young are interested in magic. People of all ages are amazed and held spellbound by amateur and professional magicians. The language of magic can be understood by the child, the adolescent, the adult, and the aged. And yet, in a truer sense, magic at its best is something that is not understood at all or only vaguely.

The mysteriousness of magic makes its appeal to our wonderment and sense of curiosity. The appeal of religion is partly due to these same elements of mystery. A religion that our finite minds could fully comprehend and analyze would leave us wholly unsatisfied. Certainly, we need a religion much bigger than our minds can grasp. The unknown and incomprehensible in religion can be illuminated and made more reasonable by these simple illustrations from the realm of magic.

Magic has a popular appeal to the child's mind. It arouses a sense of curiosity. Simple magic is used in these Junior Sermons because it is an easy way to overcome the child's indifference and disinterest. This, however, is only the by-product of magic; its real value is that each magic illustration teaches a moral and religious truth.

The materials to be used in these magic illustrations are available in any home, or may be bought in your local store for a few cents.

J. J. S.

College Point, New York.

CONTENTS

CONTENTS

8

THE NEW YEAR

Materials:

Two men's handkerchiefs (one of which is clean and the other dirty and spotted).

One small elastic or a larger one which has been doubled.

Demonstration:

The two handkerchiefs are to be knotted together. This may be done by the use of a small rubber band which the performer secretly slips over the tips of his thumb and forefinger. Use this same thumb and forefinger to hold a corner of each handkerchief. Then the two handkerchiefs are to be thrown into the air, but just before throwing them the rubber band is slipped over the two corners in your hand. The elastic will be made to slide readily from the thumb and forefinger around the two corners by spreading the two fingers. When the handkerchiefs return from the air they are seen to be mysteriously knotted together.

Then the performer takes the knotted ends in his hand and secretly removes the rubber band just before throwing them aloft for the second time. The handkerchiefs will then float down separately. As the performer stoops to pick up the separated handkerchiefs, he may drop the elastic on the floor to get rid of it.

Story:

Today we stand at the beginning of a New Year. How wonderful that seems—A NEW YEAR! We are able to begin over again. Every one of us has made mistakes during the old year—the past year. Now we have an opportunity to enter a NEW YEAR.

What a thrill when we ride in a new automobile, receive a new toy, or live in a new house. We forget all about the old automobile, the worn-out toy, and the old dilapidated house, and look forward to the new things.

But what about the NEW YEAR? Let us say that this nice clean handkerchief represents a clean page, a new beginning, a NEW YEAR. This dirty, spotted handkerchief shall represent the past year, with all its mistakes, blots, and heartaches, such as irreverence to God, disobedience to parents, failures in school, etc. Shall we take all these mistakes and failures with us into the NEW YEAR?

(The performer takes the two handkerchiefs and throws them into the air. As they come down, he catches one of them by a corner, and the other one, instead of falling to the ground, is seen to be mysteriously knotted to the one which the performer has caught.) You see we are able to take all our mistakes along with us, just as these two handkerchiefs are knotted together. Or shall we leave our mistakes behind us? (The elastic is now removed secretly as the performer talks. Once again the handkerchiefs are thrown into the air and both flutter separately to the ground, the knot having disappeared as mysteriously as it appeared in the first instance.)

Let us take this dirty, spotted handkerchief and throw it away and keep this clean, unspotted one. So

we will leave these mistakes behind and begin the NEW
YEAR with a clean, pure page. I wish that every one
of you could learn this little poem which I am going to
recite for you.

> " He came to my desk with quivering lip—
>   The Lesson was done.
> ' Dear teacher, I want a new leaf,' he said,
> ' I have spoiled this one.'
>   I took the old leaf, stained and blotted,
>   And gave him a new one, all unspotted,
>   And into his sad eyes smiled
> ' Do better, now, my child.' "

2

GOD—THE ROCK OF AGES

Materials:
   Ring.
   Handkerchief.
   Small rubber band.

Demonstration:

Get a small rubber band, or if one of a small size is
not available, use an ordinary sized one and double it
to make it smaller. The rubber band is secretly placed
over the thumb and forefinger of the left hand, and a
handkerchief is thrown over the hand to cover it. The
ring is then placed in the center of the handkerchief;
the thumb and forefinger of the left hand grasp it
through the handkerchief and slip the rubber band over
it, thus enclosing it in a little pocket, whose mouth is

closed by the rubber band. A pretense may be made of folding the handkerchief over the ring while the rubber band is being adjusted. The right hand then grasps one corner of the handkerchief, shakes it out, and the ring has vanished.

Story:

After the Hebrews had been slaves in Egypt for over four hundred years, a little baby boy was born whose name was Moses. He became a great leader, who led the Hebrews from Egypt to the Holy Land. Many adventures happened on this long journey, one of which I am going to relate.

One night the Hebrews arrived at Mt. Sinai and encamped there. It was at this place that God gave the Ten Commandments to the people. Moses went to the top of the mountain to talk with God, while the people remained below. Moses stayed on the summit for forty days.

The people became impatient, and what do you suppose they did? They took all their golden rings, their chains, their bracelets, and many other ornaments to Aaron the priest. He melted all these and from them formed a golden calf. Then the people danced and sang and worshipped this calf.

When Moses heard all this singing and noise he came down the mountain and was very angry. He smashed the stone tablets upon which the Ten Commandments were written; took the golden calf, ground it to powder, sprinkled it upon the drinking water, and compelled the people to drink it.

What happened? The golden idol and the rings disappeared, did they not? But the God who gave us the Ten Commandments is still with us.

Now let us imagine that this golden ring which I take from my finger represents all the jewelry which was brought to Aaron the priest. You remember that Moses destroyed the golden calf by grinding it to powder and mixing it with water. Shall we all watch this ring? (Perform the trick.) Why, the ring has disappeared, has it not, just as the golden calf disappeared?

You see things of this world vanish, but can you tell me who always remains forever and ever? Yes, you are right, God will always be with us. So let us worship the God who always remains and not the golden idols which will vanish as the ring did.

3

JESUS AT THE CENTER

Materials:

A piece of paper six inches square.

Demonstration:

Fold this square piece of paper so that the creases will make nine smaller squares. Write the name *Jesus* in the center square and the names of some famous people in history in the other squares, such as Washington, Lincoln, Luther, etc. Tear the paper along the creases. The nine pieces are put into a hat. With his hands behind his back and toward the audience the performer picks up each piece of paper separately, feeling the edges with the forefinger and thumb. The paper with the name *Jesus* has four ragged edges and can readily be identified by the touch, while the other pieces have one or two smooth edges.

Story:

Leonardo Da Vinci painted a very famous picture called *The Last Supper*. It shows Jesus eating His last supper with His twelve disciples. (Exhibit a copy of the painting.) Six of the disciples are on one side of Jesus and six on the other. That puts Jesus at the very center. That is the way it should be. This piece of paper (show paper) is creased so that it has nine squares. In the center square is Jesus. For us Christians Jesus should be the center of everything. This means that everything we do should be done to please Christ.

All of us want to live at some future time in a much more beautiful world than this one. That other beautiful world we call heaven. Jesus should be at the very center of our lives as He is at the center of this paper, because He is the only one who can help us get to heaven. In one of these squares is the name of Washington. He was the first president of the United States. In another square is the name of Lincoln. He set the slaves free. Washington and Lincoln were great men and they have done much for us, but they cannot get us into heaven. Only Jesus can do that.

Of all the people who have ever lived or are still living you must pick Jesus as your guide and helper. It should be the most natural thing to want Jesus to help us. Let us see if, without looking, I can pick Jesus from among the others on this sheet of paper. (Tear paper along creases and perform trick.) Yes, I succeeded in choosing Jesus. I only hope that we will all succeed in choosing Jesus for our daily living.

Much in life is important but the most important of all is Jesus. There is a fable of a fox and a cat who one day were talking together in the forest. The fox

said to the cat: " Whatever happens, I am safe, for I
have a thousand tricks by which to escape from hunters
and dogs." " Alas," said the cat, " I have only one
way of escape, and I hope that this way will never fail."
Just then a pack of hounds came rushing through the
woods. The cat used her one way of escape by climb-
ing a tree. But the poor fox, with his thousand tricks,
found not one that would help him. He was killed by
the dogs. It is not important for us to know a thousand
tricks. These cannot help us. But it is very important
that we know Jesus. He can help us. He should be
at the very center of our lives.

4

THE SPIRIT OF GOD

Materials:

A lump of sugar.
A soft pencil.
A glass of warm water.

Demonstration:

With a soft pencil mark the letter " G " on a lump
of sugar. Hold the sugar with your thumb firmly over
the letter to obtain an impression of it. Drop the sugar
in a glass of water. Then take the hand of your helper
whom you have called on to assist you, and hold it
over the glass. Press your thumb, on which you have
an impression of the letter, firmly on the palm of his
hand over the glass, until the sugar is melted. The
letter on the lump of dissolved sugar seems to have
passed magically to the palm of his hand.

Story:

In the very beginning there was no earth. Then God created the earth, but there was nothing but darkness and water upon it. Then something happened: the Spirit of God moved over the earth. Now there was light, light everywhere. The sun gave light and heat in the daytime, and the moon and stars shone at night. Dry land appeared, and the green grass began to grow, the fruit trees to blossom, and the flowers to bloom. Then God made all the animals, the birds and the fish. And, finally, He made man.

The earth would not have become lovely and beautiful with grass, flowers, and trees if God's Spirit had not moved over the earth. The Spirit of God can do everything. Although it is so strong, you cannot see it; you can only feel it. Jesus told Nicodemus that the Spirit of God was like the wind—you can feel it but not see it. You have felt the wind blowing through your hair; perhaps you have seen it blow down trees and houses, or you may have seen it whip the ocean into huge waves. Yet you cannot see the wind; you cannot hold it in your hands. God's Spirit is like that. When it moved over the earth it could not be seen, but it made the earth beautiful.

We are not lovely and beautiful unless God's Spirit makes us so. We can have His Spirit in our hearts even if we cannot see it. (Perform trick.) This lump of sugar has on it the letter " G," which stands for God. (Then place thumb over the letter firmly to get the impression.) I will drop it into this glass of water, where it will dissolve and you cannot see it. (Hold your helper's hand over the glass with your thumb pressed firmly into the palm of his hand. The letter on the dissolved piece of sugar seems to have passed magically to his hand.) But look! The letter " G," which we said stood for God, and which disappeared in the water, is now in the palm of your hand. So the Spirit of God, which you cannot see, can be in your heart. If you let it come into your heart, it will make your life lovely and beautiful.

5

PRAYER—A HELP

Materials:

An ordinary piece of paper.
A candle.
A piece of paper which has been dipped into alum water a number of times.

Demonstration:

Prepare paper by dipping three times for some duration in a strong solution of alum water. Let it dry, and repeat this at least twice. Put into flame of candle, and it will not burn. An ordinary piece of paper also is necessary.

Story:

Many years ago, in a far-away country, the land of Babylonia, there ruled a king named Nebuchadnezzar. In his kingdom there lived four Hebrew boys. You probably have heard of Daniel, especially the story when he was in the lions' den. Daniel had three friends, who had very odd names, Shadrach, Meshach, and Abednego.

King Nebuchadnezzar made an image of gold and set

it up on the plain; then he commanded a herald to go
through the streets in the city.   This herald called:
"Hear ye! Hear ye! When ye hear the sound of
the cornet, flute, harp and all kinds of music, ye must
fall down and pray to the golden image that Nebuchadnezzar hath set up and whosoever doth not fall
down and worship, shall the very same hour be thrown
into a fiery furnace."

When the trumpets sounded, all people fell on their
knees. Did I say all? No, not all. Shadrach, Meshach,
and Abednego would not pray to this image, this idol.
Then the king was angry and he commanded his
servants to heat the furnace seven times hotter than it
usually was.   Then these three friends were bound and
thrown into the furnace.

But did they burn?   No! they prayed to God, and
because they had been true to Him, God did not allow
the fire to harm even one hair on their heads. So, you
see, God helped them because they prayed to Him instead of to the idol.

Now, will you watch carefully?   The Bible tells us
that when the king's servants put Shadrach, Meshach
and Abednego into the furnace, the fire was so hot that
it burned the servants.   Do you see this sheet of paper?   It is just a common, ordinary piece of writing
paper.   What will happen if we put it into the candle
flame?   Watch!   Yes, it burns.   You see, it is only a
piece of writing paper which cannot resist the fire.
Neither could the servants stand the great heat, for
they did not trust in nor pray to God.

But look at this piece of paper.   It has been treated
so that the flames will not hurt it.   Let us put it into the
candle flame.   See, it does not burn, does it?   Why not?
It has been treated so that it cannot be destroyed by

fire. I dipped it into alum water, and alum does not burn. Boys and girls who pray to God are treated by God in such a way that no harm or evil shall come upon them. God takes care of the children who pray to Him. Shadrach, Meshach and Abednego did not burn, because they prayed to God, and He protected them.

Shall we try to be like Shadrach, Meshach and Abednego? Let us all ask God to help us and protect us.

6

GOD IN US

Materials:

Two pieces of rope, each about eight feet long.
A piece of yarn about four inches long.
A candle.

Demonstration:

Use two small ropes about eight feet long. Prepare for trick by laying ropes down, loops at center, two ends out each way, tying ropes together with yarn or any string which will break easily. Place the ropes around your body, with tied place in the center of your back. Have two helpers, one to your right and the other to your left, take hold of the ends, warning them not to pull. Then under pretense of making trick more difficult, exchange the ends of the rope, giving the helper on the right one of the rope ends from the left and vice versa. Then ask the helpers to pull gently and together. The yarn will now break and the ropes will apparently have passed through your body.

Story:

Have you seen the wind? You have seen the wind blow dust or blow dry leaves, but you have not seen the wind. (Blow at the flame of the candle.) You could see the flame flicker and move back and forth because I blew it, but you could not see the wind. You can feel the wind, but you cannot see it.

How much is two and two? Four. That is right. How do you know that four is correct? You just know. It is in your mind; in your brain. How did it get into your mind? You did not see it go in, did you? No! But it is there just the same. You did not see the wind, but the wind moved the flame just the same.

One of our great presidents was Abraham Lincoln. When he was a young man, he worked in a grocery store. One day, when a lady was buying groceries, Lincoln made a mistake; he did not give the lady enough change. It was only a few pennies, but he walked several miles that night to give her the pennies. He could have kept them, because the lady did not miss them. Lincoln was honest. Lincoln's honesty was right in his heart. Did anyone see it go in there? No! You did not see the wind, but the wind moved the flame just the same.

Here I have two ropes. (Put ropes around your body as told in explanation.) If you pull on them they should become tighter and tighter around my body, should they not? If you pull hard enough the ropes might even pass through my body. That's just what we will do. (Now ask the two helpers to pull gently and together, and the ropes will seem to have passed through your body.) Did you see the ropes go through my body? No! Did anyone see the wind? (Blow the candle.) No! Did anyone see that " two and two equal four " go into your brain? No! Did anyone see honesty go into Lincoln's heart? No!

God is in your hearts. Did anyone see Him go in there? No! You did not see Him go in there. You can feel God as you can feel the wind, but you cannot see Him. (Blow at the candle once more.) Yes, if the candle had eyes, could it see the wind? No! But the wind is there, even if the candle cannot see it. God is in our hearts, even if we cannot see Him. We know He is there because we can feel Him there.

7

BRINGING CHRIST TO OTHERS
(MISSIONS)

Materials:

A piece of elastic about eighteen inches long.

Two pencils, one black and the other white.

A large white handkerchief and a piece of black material about the same size.

Demonstration:

Run an elastic up your sleeve and fasten one end to your vest and the other end to the black pencil, which you hold upright in your hand. This pencil can be held naturally and in such a way that the elastic is not visible. Throw the black material over the pencil so that it drapes over the entire hand. When the material is removed, the black pencil is still there. Now hold the white pencil beside the black one. Drape the white handkerchief over both pencils and, while the hand is covered, release the black pencil and the elastic will pull it up your sleeve. When the handkerchief is removed only the white pencil remains. If the shirt sleeve is rolled up, under the coat, the black pencil will have less interference as it slides up the coat sleeve.

Story:

The people who live in the far places of the world all have religion. Their religion is very much different from that of the Christian religion. We Christians know that many of them have the wrong kind of religion. We send missionaries to them to bring them our Christ and the Christian religion.

Many of them are very superstitious. What does superstition mean? If you believe that a rabbit's foot or a horseshoe can bring you good luck then you are superstitious. Some think that walking under a ladder or breaking a mirror will bring them bad luck. That is all foolishness; that is superstition.

This black pencil stands for superstition. (Hold it upright.) Superstition is black ignorance and that is why I chose a black pencil.

In far-away Arabia many believe that there is such a thing as an Evil Eye to hurt you. The Evil Eye is supposed to be able to cast a spell on you and bring you bad luck. Arab mothers are very much afraid of it. When they see a stranger coming they cover up their babies so he can't send the Evil Eye to hurt their little ones. And the men think that they have to protect themselves from the Evil Eye in their business. To keep away the spell of the Evil Eye they wear old coins hanging from their ears, and around the neck they carry holy earth in a bag trimmed with blue beads.

That is superstition. They are so superstitious because they have the wrong religion. Their religion keeps them that way. Their religion is as black as this cloth. (Drape it over the pencil and hand.) They live under the black ignorance of their religion.

In far-away Japan there are large temples. If we could follow a Japanese worshipper into the temple, what would we see? Perhaps he may buy a prayer written on paper and then go to a big stone idol. Then he will put the paper into his mouth and chew it into a wet ball. Then kneeling, he will bow until his forehead touches the floor. Finally, he will throw the wet ball at the idol. If the wet paper prayer sticks to the idol the prayer will be answered, but if it does not the idol is displeased. That is superstition and those people are that way because of their religion.

(Point to black material covering black pencil.) We must give them a better religion than that. (Remove black material and place white pencil beside the black one.) This white pencil stands for Christ. I chose a white pencil because Christ is pure and white in His heart. White stands also for light, and Christ is the light of the world. Our missionaries are sent to those superstitious people to bring them our Christ. And when Christ (point to white pencil) is placed next to their idols and superstition (point to black pencil) they will eventually disappear.

We must bring our Christianity to them. (Drape white handkerchief over both pencils and the hand.) This white handkerchief stands for Christianity, which, at its best, is clean, white, and pure. When we bring our Christ and our Christianity to people whose religion is wrong, their idols and superstitions will some day disappear altogether. (Release the black pencil and let it slide up the sleeve; remove white handkerchief; point

to white pencil.)   They will worship our God as we
know Him through Christ.

8

THE SALT OF THE EARTH

Materials:

An egg.

One glass pure water.

One glass salt water.   (A strong salt solution.   To
avoid cloudiness do not use free-running salt.)

Demonstration:

Egg in pure water sinks to the bottom of the glass.
The egg in the salt water floats.

Story:

Jesus often told His friends stories which were difficult to understand.   One day He said, " Ye are the salt
of the earth."   Was it not a strange thing to say?
How could His friends or our friends or we ourselves be
salt?   Yet Jesus said, " Ye are the salt of the earth."

Now, will you all watch me carefully?   Think while
you are watching.   (First put egg into pure water and
then in the salt water.)   Now isn't that strange?   Both
of the glasses of water look the same, but the same egg
acts differently.   Shall I tell you why?   One glass contains pure water and the other one salt water.   In the
pure water the egg sinks to the bottom of the glass, but
the salt water lifts it up.

Ah! there we have the secret.   Salt lifts.   Jesus said,

" Ye are the salt of the earth." So we, like salt, must lift. But how can we lift? I will tell you.

If we see some one who is sad we must make him happy. Smile and soon there will be a mile of smiles. Suppose some one is ill, how can we lift him? Let us wait on him, run errands for him, do whatever we can to make him well and happy.

One day I saw a little girl about four years of age trying to cross the street. A boy of ten years of age came along and noticed that she was in trouble. He took her by the hand and helped her across. He was " salt," was he not?

Whenever we see some boy or girl who uses bad language, is dirty, careless, or unkind, let us show that boy or girl a better way. Then we will be like salt and lift up. So remember that it was Jesus who said, " Ye are the salt of the earth."

9

OVERCOMING HANDICAPS

Materials:

A handkerchief, preferably a silk one.

Demonstration:

Tie a loose knot in the center of the handkerchief. Make the knot disappear, not by untying it, but by drawing your hand over it. Draw your hand over it several times without making the knot vanish. When you are ready to make it disappear, catch your thumb in a fold of the knot, and as your hand descends, pull it off to the end of the handkerchief. The thumb caught in the fold will not be detected, since it is covered by the fingers and the back of the hand.

Story:

All of us have some kind of handicaps. What is a handicap? A handicap is a disadvantage. What is a disadvantage? A disadvantage may keep you from succeeding. For example, if a person cannot hear well that is called a handicap. The fact that he cannot hear well may keep him from succeeding. But he need not be a failure. That all depends upon the person. He can overcome his handicap. Ludwig van Beethoven became deaf when he was still a very young man. He did not say: " I can't do anything worth while because I am deaf." He became one of the greatest musical composers whom the world has ever seen. He could not even hear the music that he composed. That certainly was a handicap. He consulted many doctors, but none could help him. Then Beethoven faced his terrible handicap with courage. His deafness was not going to get him down and discouraged. He worked at his music harder than ever, and when he was composing, he would scarcely eat for days at a time. He would bend very low over the keys of his piano trying to catch the sound. Even though he was deaf, he led the orchestra that played the music which he wrote. When the people showed their appreciation by applause, he could not even hear this. In spite of sickness, poverty, and deafness, Beethoven continued to write music that made him, perhaps, the greatest composer who ever lived. There was a man who overcame his handicaps.

(Show handkerchief with knot.) This knot we will call a handicap. Sometimes when we have something difficult to do and we do not know just how to do it, we say, "This is a knotty problem." Beethoven had many "knotty problems" in his life. He was sick, he was poor, he was deaf. But Beethoven untied the knots; he overcame his handicaps. Here is a knot in this handkerchief. I will take out the knot in the easiest way I know how. (Perform the trick.) Well, this knot seems to have come out by itself. I did not even untie it. Beethoven did not overcome his handicaps that easily. It was done by hard work and by trying again and again.

Look at Jesus. Did He have any handicaps? Yes, indeed. He was poor. He came from a small, despised town. The people said: "He comes from Nazareth; nothing good ever comes out of Nazareth." They said: "We know His parents; they are just poor peasants." It was an uphill struggle for Jesus. An uphill climb is a real handicap. But such handicaps make some people all the more determined to make good. Jesus would not turn back even if they killed Him. And that is just what they did. They nailed Him to a cross. But today we know that Jesus was right and those who killed Him were wrong.

Handicaps are obstacles in the way. Jesus had obstacles in the way; so did Beethoven; so have we. These obstacles are like the knot in the handkerchief. Steinmetz was a cripple but he became a great scientist. Robert Louis Stevenson was sick all his life but he wrote many books and stories. We must take out the knots, overcome the handicaps, and go on. We must not let handicaps whip and beat us. The knot in the handkerchief seems to have come out by itself or by magic, but not so with handicaps. We must work and fight to overcome them.

10

THE JOY OF GIVING

Materials:

Two pencils.

A stone about the size of an egg.

A sponge filled with water in a dish.

Demonstration:

Show how impossible it is to squeeze water from a rock. Then take one of the pencils in your fist so that the lead points downward. Bring this fist up to your ear. This will bring the elbow up, and pointing directly at your helper, ask him to trace very slowly with his finger a cross on your elbow. Bring your hand down and try to squeeze water from the pencil without success. Then lift the sponge and show how easy it is to squeeze water from it. Now take the other pencil, or, still better, borrow one from the audience to avoid the suspicion that your pencil has a secret water chamber. Hold it as you held the first pencil. As you bring the hand that holds it to your ear, ask your helper to make the cross on your elbow. While the attention of the audience is on the cross he traces, you remove from behind your ear, where it was secretly placed, a wad of soft tissue paper that has been thoroughly soaked with water. Take your hand down and as you squeeze the wad and the pencil in the one hand, water will be seen dripping from the end of the pencil.

Story:

God is always giving. He gives to us every day.

He gives us sunshine and rain. If He did not give us
rain and sunshine nothing would grow and we would all
die of hunger. He gives us coal to heat our houses.
He put this coal deep in the earth and all we have to
do is to get it. He gives us life. We would not even
be here if God had not given us life. He has given us
eyes with which to see, and ears with which to hear.
God is not happy unless He gives.

We, too, will be happy if we give as God does. God
is happy when He makes us happy. We, too, will be
happy when we make others happy. Jesus was always
giving. He gave health to the sick, food to the hungry,
and cheer to those in trouble.

Jesus said that the person who was willing to give
his life for another had the greatest love in the world.
That is exactly what Jesus Himself did. God sent
Jesus to this earth. Then Jesus told us how God wants
us to live. But there were many people who did not
want to live that way. They got together and told
Jesus that they would kill Him if He interfered with
them. But Jesus loved the people and He told them
what God wanted them to do. So His enemies nailed
Him to a cross. Jesus loved us enough to give His life.
He died for us.

If Jesus loved us so much that He gave His life, don't
you think that we, too, ought to give? On our churches
we often see crosses, and many people have little
crosses on their watch chains, or on chains around their
necks. Why? The cross reminds them of how much
Jesus gave; He gave His life.

God is greatly pleased when we give something to
others. There are some people who never give anything. They have a hard heart, a heart like stone. A
person with such a heart will not give. Some one has

said of a stingy person, " You can't squeeze water from a rock." Here is a rock. (Squeeze it.) No matter how hard I squeeze, it will not give any water. Some people are like this rock.

Charles Dickens told of a man called Ebenezer Scrooge who never gave anything. Even on Christmas day, when others gave presents, he gave nothing. He thought only of his business and how to get more money. He had no time to make others happy. As a result, he was a lonely man and no one liked him. But, finally, his heart became soft, and he started to give to others, and not until then was he happy.

Here is a pencil. I wonder whether we can squeeze water from it. I will ask my helper to make a cross on my elbow. When this pencil sees the cross, which reminds us of how much Jesus gave, perhaps the pencil, too, will give. (Squeeze pencil.) No, I cannot make this pencil give anything. Some people are like this pencil; they are selfish and will not give and so they are unhappy.

But there are many people who are like this sponge. (Squeeze sponge.) It is easy for them to give, just as this sponge gives water. They like to give; it makes them happy.

Mr. William Colgate, who made Colgate soap and tooth paste, was a good Christian. Of every dollar that he earned he finally gave one-half to God for the Church and needy people. The more he gave, the more God blessed him. Mr. Colgate was like this pencil. (Take second pencil or borrow one from the audience, and have helper put cross on your elbow.) When Mr. Colgate saw the cross, he was reminded of how much Jesus had given and this made it a pleasure for him to give. (Squeeze pencil.) Mr. Colgate was

like this pencil. He gave gladly. We may not have so
much to give as Mr. Colgate, but we can all give something. It is not the amount we give, but whether we
give gladly.

11

THE MONSTER OF SIN

Materials:

Two small match boxes.

Demonstration:

To prepare for this demonstration, remove the label
from one match box and paste it on the bottom of the
other. The top and the bottom of the prepared box will
then be identical. Remove all the matches. Break
down the bottom of the drawer just enough so that you
can put a card of the proper size between the bottom
of the drawer and the bottom of the box. On this card
draw the picture of a snake. Over the snake write the
word " sin." Holding the box right side up, partly open
the drawer and show the audience that it is empty.
Have some one come forward to make a close inspection to see that it is empty. Then, when you open the
box again, this time with the bottom side of the drawer
up, the audience will be surprised to find the card. If
you will occasionally turn the box in your hand as you
talk and before you open the drawer to show when it
is empty and when not, it will prevent the audience
from detecting that the box has been especially prepared. You should have a secret mark on the box in
order to know which side is which.

Story:

The other day I read a strange story about a head-fish. This monster is a dangerous-looking creature, with three rows of needle-sharp teeth on each jaw. Although this fish lives only in the deep sea, where do you suppose this one was found? It was found dead and floating in a pond near Rumson, New Jersey. This pond is quite a number of miles away from the ocean. It has no connection with the ocean, and there are no streams flowing into it. It is fed by springs. And in this sweet, fresh water was found this monster, which, according to its size, was fifty years old. The owner of the pond raised ducks every year, and then, before long, they would disappear one after the other. He could not understand what was happening to the ducks. So this year he put a ten-foot fence around the pond, thinking that in this way he could keep the ducks. But still they disappeared. Now he knows why he lost the ducks. The monster headfish caught them as they were swimming on the water, and then ate them. But the question is, How did this monster get into that pond? No one knows.

(Show the empty drawer of the match box.) When God first made the world it was empty, like this box. There were no trees, flowers, or grass. There were no animals. There were no people. And then God made all these and put them into this world. The name of the first man was Adam, and the first woman was called Eve. They lived happily together, and they did not know what it was to do any wrong. Then suddenly a monster came into this world, and its name is Sin. (Open the match-box drawer and produce the card.) I thought that this box was empty. But here is a card I found in it. (Ask your helper what kind of an ani-

mal is on it and what is written over it.)   How did the
card get into this box?   How did the monster headfish
get into the pond?   How did the monster Sin get into
the world to make Adam and Eve unhappy?   God told
Adam and Eve not to eat the fruit from one tree in the
garden.   But, according to the Bible story, a snake
told them to eat the fruit even though God had told
them not to do it.   And they did eat the fruit.   They
disobeyed God.   To disobey God, that is sin.   Because
they disobeyed, God would not allow them to live in
the garden any longer.   Sin had made them unhappy;
it always makes people unhappy.

Sin is a monster.   We don't know how that monster
headfish got into the pond, but we know that it was
there, and that it not only made much trouble for the
ducks, but killed as many as it could.   We don't know
how the monster Sin got into the world but it is here,
and not only tries to make us unhappy, but would
destroy us if it could.

Sin tells us that we can tell lies if we want to, that
if we see anything we want we should just steal it, that
if there is something that does not suit us we should get
very angry and say mean things that hurt.   That is
what Sin does.

A headfish is not nearly so bad as Sin.   We can see
the headfish and get away from it.   But the monster
Sin we cannot see.   We cannot see it any more than
we can see air.   But air is very real; it is all around
us.   Sin, too, is very real, and although we cannot see
it, it is always whispering in our ears to do the things
that we should not do, and then we are unhappy.   The
best thing we can do is not to listen to Sin.   Instead, let
us listen to God.   He tells us the good things that we
ought to do.   And if we do these, then we are happy.

12

ARE YOU SORRY?

Materials:

A man's clean handkerchief.

Demonstration:

The performer holds the handkerchief by one corner between right thumb and fingers. He takes in his left hand the lower corner diagonally opposite the one he is holding, shows it to the audience, and places this corner also in his right hand. With a quick snap he releases it, still holding the corner which he held originally. Nothing out of the ordinary has happened, so he repeats the same process a second and a third time, when a knot magically appears in the lower corner.

Before showing the trick, the performer ties a knot in one corner of the handkerchief. This corner is held in the right hand, the knot being hidden behind the fingers. The first two times the handkerchief is shaken out, the lower or opposite corner is released. On the third shake, the lower corner is retained in the right hand and the knotted corner is released.

Story:

How many of you have a good friend? Yes, I think we all have at least one dear friend, haven't we?

When Jesus was here on earth He had twelve friends. I am going to tell you about two of them. One of these friends was Judas. Judas loved Jesus and was with Him continually; but, you know, Judas came to love something else better and this was money. Now, not everyone loved Jesus and believed in Him. No, there were some people who wished to kill Him. So Judas went to some of these enemies of Jesus and said, " If you give me thirty pieces of silver, I will tell you where you may find Jesus and then you can capture Him." So the enemies agreed to pay Judas the thirty pieces of silver and Judas sold his best friend, Jesus. He wasn't even sorry for what he had done.

Now let us look at the second friend of Jesus called Peter. Peter also loved Jesus, but one day something happened. You remember that Judas sold Jesus for thirty pieces of silver, don't you? The enemies now had made Jesus a prisoner. Peter was standing near by at a fire warming his hands. Some one came up to him and said, " Peter, you are Jesus' friend, aren't you? " What do you suppose Peter said? " Yes "? Oh, no! He said: " Why, I don't even know the man." He even repeated this a second and a third time. Then looking around, he saw Jesus. Oh, how sorry he was! He went away and wept.

Do you see this handkerchief? It's nice and clean and white, is it not? At first, Judas's life was clean and pure, just like this handkerchief. (Shake handkerchief out twice but retain knot in hand.) But when Judas betrayed Jesus, what happened? (Cause knot to appear as you shake out the handkerchief for the third time.) Yes, a knot appeared in his life and remained because he was not sorry.

(Before beginning demonstration on Peter's life pretend to remove knot from handkerchief but actually retain knot in hand.) Peter's life also was as pure and clean as this handkerchief. Now, when Peter denied Jesus, a knot also appeared in his life. (Demonstrate with handkerchief as you did in the case of Judas.)

But you remember that Peter was sorry, was he not? (Cause knot to disappear by shaking handkerchief and retaining knot in right hand.) See, Jesus forgave Peter just as this knot has disappeared.

Boys and girls, if we tell a lie, disobey our parents or do wrong, whom will we be like, Judas, who was not sorry, or Peter, who asked for forgiveness?

13

A GREAT WELCOME THAT TURNED INTO A TRAGEDY

(PALM SUNDAY)

Materials:

A cylinder ten inches long and two inches in diameter, made of corrugated cardboard and rolled so that it will have double walls.

A piece of elastic about eighteen inches long.

Two small silk handkerchiefs, one white and the other red.

Demonstration:

In making the cylinder, roll the red handkerchief between the two walls. At one end leave just enough of the handkerchief exposed so that it will not be visible to the audience and yet enough so that it can be extracted. Hold this end toward you and away from the audience. Allow the audience to look through the cylinder. The white handkerchief is well fastened to one end of the elastic. This elastic is run up the right sleeve and the other end fastened to the vest. You appear before the audience with the white handkerchief in your right hand. There should be enough strain on the elastic so that when you let go of the handkerchief it will slip up your sleeve. Push the white handkerchief into the cylinder and hold the ends of it between the palms of the hands. Release the cylinder a trifle from the right palm and the white handkerchief will be drawn up the sleeve. Exhibit the empty cylinder. Now draw the red handkerchief from between the walls of the cylinder. To the astonishment of the audience, the white handkerchief has mysteriously disappeared and the red one is produced from the empty cylinder.

Story:

On the morning of May 20, 1927, Charles A. Lindbergh did a daring thing. He set out to do something that had never been done before, to cross the Atlantic Ocean from New York to Paris. That dark night, while he was flying through the clouds, sleet began to form on his plane. The weight of too much ice on the plane would have forced it into the sea. Then Lindbergh decided to fly around and over the clouds. On and on, he flew through the night, all alone, with no sound save the roar of his engine. Would he have enough gasoline to get to Paris? Finally, when he saw a small fishing vessel, he knew that he was near Europe. He flew over Ireland and England, and went on to France, where he landed safely. He had made the trip in thirty-three hours and thirty minutes. Lindbergh became the hero of the world, and the hero of every boy and girl. When he returned to the United States, he received the greatest welcome that any person in history had ever received. When he came to New York City and rode up Broadway, the city went wild with cheers, and confetti and paper streamers were strewn from the windows of the tall buildings so that it looked like a snowstorm.

About two thousand years ago a much more important welcome was given to Jesus as He entered the city of Jerusalem. It was the fourth day before the Jewish celebration of the Passover. The celebration of the Passover is to Jews what Easter is to us. Great crowds had gathered in the city to celebrate. Most of them were talking about Jesus of Nazareth because He had done such wonderful things. He had healed the sick, given sight to the blind, hearing to the deaf, and He had just brought Lazarus to life. So, when Jesus came near to the city, riding on a donkey, a great crowd went out to meet Him. Branches were torn from palm trees and waved with enthusiasm. That is why we call this day Palm Sunday. " Hosanna, blessed is he that cometh in the name of the Lord," was joyously shouted by the crowd.

Here is a white handkerchief. (Exhibit it.) White stands for purity, peace, and joy. This peace-loving and joyful crowd followed Jesus into the city. Jesus' destination was the temple. Here, at the entrance, were merchants selling goods at exorbitant prices, and that in such a holy place as the temple. What a sin that was! Jesus drove them out, which naturally made them very angry. The scribes and Pharisees did not like Jesus either. These enemies of Jesus got together and stirred up the people against Him. Then the crowd started shouting, " Crucify him." Where was that welcoming crowd? (Allow white handkerchief to slip up your sleeve and exhibit empty cylinder.) The happy, peaceful crowd was gone just as the white handkerchief has disappeared.

So angry was this crowd that they wanted to kill
Jesus. They became red with anger. (Produce red
handkerchief.) They shouted over and over, " Crucify
him."

This peaceful, happy Palm Sunday crowd changed
into a wild mob, and finally led Jesus to Calvary's hill
to be crucified on the day which we now observe as
Good Friday.

14

THE BROKEN CHRIST
(Good Friday)

Materials:

A large handkerchief.
Two matches.

Demonstration:

First, you must conceal a match in the hem of the
handkerchief. Mark the other match with a drop of
ink and show it to the spectators. You need a helper.
Fold the marked match in the handkerchief. Fold the
handkerchief in such a way as to bring the match in
the hem into position, so that it may be broken by the
helper, and protect the marked match with your hands.
Then shake out handkerchief and from it produce the
marked, unbroken match.

Story:

Many, many years ago the country of Palestine, the
Holy Land, was ruled by the Romans. The Roman
governor in the time of Jesus was called Pilate. The

Jewish rulers in those days hated Jesus and continually tried to find a reason for killing Him. Finally they accused Jesus of treason against the Roman government and brought Him to Pilate, the governor, to be judged. Pilate listened to the witnesses against Jesus, and after hearing them all, he said, " I find no fault with Jesus." So the Jews who sought for Jesus' death saw that they would have to use other methods. Therefore, they said to Pilate, " If you release Jesus, you are not Cæsar's friend; we'll tell Cæsar about you and you will lose your position."

Then Pilate thought that he would make one more effort. The Roman government in those days had a custom of setting free one prisoner at the time of the Jewish Feast of the Passover. It was now Passover week. Pilate remembered that there was a wicked prisoner in jail named Barabbas. So he thought, " I'll give these Jews their choice of freeing Jesus or Barabbas, and I am sure that they will free Jesus because Barabbas is such a wicked man."

So Pilate gave the Jews their choice. But, to his surprise, they chose to free Barabbas and to crucify Jesus. So Jesus, the innocent, was led away to be crucified. After Jesus' death, He was put into a tomb. (Fold match in handkerchief.) Jesus died on the cross, His body was broken for us. He Himself said, " This is my body, broken for you." (Have helper break match.) Now that Jesus was dead, everyone thought He was no longer on earth. But listen to the end of the story. Early on Sunday morning His broken body was no longer in the tomb. He was again on earth (exhibit marked match), and He is with us today and will be with us always. Jesus said: " I am with you always, even unto the end of the world."

15

THE RESURRECTION OF JESUS

Materials:

One small tumbler.
A glass disc the size of the bottom of the tumbler.
A handkerchief.
A quarter.

Demonstration:

Fill the tumbler with water and place the handkerchief over it. Hold the quarter between thumb and forefinger and the concealed disc in one hand, and then place that hand under the handkerchief. You must now exchange the genuine coin for the glass disc under the handkerchief. As the latter is concealed in the palm of your hand, this will be a simple matter. To satisfy the audience that you still have the coin underneath the handkerchief, you allow some one to feel the glass disc through the handkerchief. While this is done you must contrive to slip the genuine coin into your pocket. You allow the glass disc to drop into the tumbler so that it can be heard distinctly as it drops. Now remove the handkerchief, and, to the surprise of every one, the coin has completely vanished. The glass disc will be unnoticed at the bottom of the tumbler, and you can even dramatically pour the water out of the glass and the disc will remain at the bottom of the tumbler. To make the trick still more interesting, you could arrange to secrete another coin of the same denomination in some unexpected spot and from there command it to appear.

Story:

This morning I will tell you a happy story, the happiest story in the whole world. Do you remember how wicked people had nailed Jesus to a cross and how on that cross He had died? Then how sad all of Jesus' friends were. They took His body and wrapped it in linen clothes, laid it in a tomb (grave), and rolled an immense stone before the opening. Near the rock stood soldiers guarding, so that no one could approach the grave without being seen.

All that night, the next day, and the following night soldiers watched there. Then something wonderful happened—there was an earthquake. The earth trembled and shook. There was a great noise, and the soldiers ran away because they were afraid. Then an angel came down from heaven and rolled away the stone from the door of the tomb.

While this wonderful thing was happening, some women, friends of Jesus, were walking slowly and sorrowfully toward the tomb. They were bringing fresh spices with which to anoint the body of Jesus. What do you suppose they saw when they came near the cave where Jesus was buried? Yes, the stone was rolled away and an angel was sitting upon it. They could scarcely believe that what they saw was true. The women were frightened. But the angel said to them: " Do not be afraid, you are looking for Jesus, are you not? But he is not here, he is risen. He is alive. Go tell his disciples." (Perform trick.)

The friends of Jesus put His body into the tomb just as we dropped this coin into the tumbler. The disciples did not find Jesus' body in the tomb, neither do we see the coin in the glass, although we are certain it was put there. As the real quarter is not in the tumbler, so the real Jesus had escaped from the tomb. He had arisen and is alive.

16

TO LIVE FOREVER
(EASTER)

Materials:

Two pieces of white ribbon about one foot long and a quarter-inch wide.

Demonstration:

Fold one piece of ribbon into inch and a half lengths and force it beneath the finger ring on the inside of the hand and leave a loose end pointing toward the finger tips. If the ring finger and the fingers on either side of it are held together with the palm toward you, the audience will not discover the ribbon. The hand can be used in a normal way, leaving the index finger and the thumb free. Show the other ribbon to the audience, cut it into several pieces and burn them in a dish. Take the ashes, rub them between the palms of your hands, catch hold of the loose end of the ribbon under the ring and draw it over the tips of your fingers. The burned ribbon seems to have been restored miraculously.

Story:

A man in the Old Testament asked a question which Jesus came to answer. The question is this: " If a man die, shall he live again? " People have always sort of half believed that man shall live in another life after this life. We all want to live forever.

The American Indians believed in a life after this one. They did not believe that when a man's body is buried he is destroyed forever. So they put into the grave such things as bows and arrows, tomahawks, beads, and, sometimes, even his horse, thinking that he could use them in the next world. In all countries and among all peoples it has been believed that man will live again after this life.

But there have always been some people and there are such today who are not certain about it, and others say that it is impossible. They want the question answered which Job asked: " If a man die, shall he live again? " Of course, God knows that a man will live again, but how was He to tell them? He sent Jesus from heaven to tell us that there is a life after this one. He proved it to us by rising from the grave. After His death He appeared to His disciples a number of times in different places.

One day, in the fall, a worm was crawling up the side of a tree. It went out on a branch and spun a cocoon to escape the cold north wind. Somewhat later the soft snowflakes fell on the cocoon and sleet encrusted it. Finally, spring came, but the worm slept on. The warm raindrops came down, tapping softly on the cocoon. And when the sun became warmer and shone upon the cocoon, the worm inside began to stir. It crawled out into the warm sunshine through a hole in one end. It stretched itself and, as it did so, beautiful wings spread out. It moved its graceful wings back and forth. It was no longer a worm; it was a beautiful butterfly. It flew up and up into the bright sunshine. The ugly worm had become a butterfly.

The worm went into the cocoon, not to die there; he came out much more beautiful. Jesus went into the tomb, not to stay there; He came out to live again. Godly and good Christian people die here, only to be more beautiful and happier in the next world.

If you burn a piece of wood, all you have left is a little ashes. If the body is burned, only ashes are left. I have here a nice white ribbon. (Cut it and burn it in the dish.) Now it is only ashes. (Rub the ashes between your hands.) But our souls are not ashes; they will live forever. (Pull out ribbon from beneath ring.)

Two boys told their father about a haunted house. To prove that the house was not haunted, the father slept in it one night. Next morning the two boys were anxious to hear what their father had to say. He said, " I did not hear a sound all night. I have not been harmed, I slept soundly." The children feared the haunted house, but the father returned safely. We need not fear the grave. Jesus returned safely to live again. He said, " Because I live, ye too shall live."

17

WHAT WE CAN TAKE TO HEAVEN

Materials:

Two matches.
A piece of cloth an inch square.
A handkerchief.
A small piece of wood.
A grain of corn or wheat.
A dime.
A small cube of bread.

Demonstration:

One of the matches has been secretly put into the hem of the handkerchief. Spread out the handkerchief on the table. Take the other match and pretend that you are rolling it up in one corner. In reality, you palm it. So that there is no doubt in the mind of your helper allow him to feel the match inside the handkerchief. The match he feels is the one hidden in the hem. Take the dime from your pocket. This gives you the opportunity to leave the palmed match in your pocket. Roll in the dime, then the bread, the cloth, the wood, and the grain. When the handkerchief is unrolled, all the objects are there except the match.

Story:

In church we often speak about heaven. Jesus spoke about heaven, and He said that He would go there to get a place ready for us. Jesus will have a place ready for all those who want to go there. I have never met a person who did not want to go to heaven. Every one here wants to go there. The one person who has made heaven, as He has made this earth and everything else, is God. The best way for us to get to heaven is to know God. Therefore, we should come to church to learn about God, read the Bible, and pray. The first person we will meet in heaven is God. We will not get to heaven if we do not know Him.

We shall also see Jesus there. He will prepare a place for us in heaven IF we ask Him to do so. Shortly before Jesus left this earth to go to heaven a man who had been a thief and a robber asked Jesus not to forget him. And Jesus told him that He would have a place ready for him.

People do not live on this earth forever. Some day we shall leave here, and not any of the things we have here can we take with us to heaven.

Jesus told a story about a very rich man who had everything he wanted. (Hold up the match.) This match, we shall say, was that rich man. (Spread handkerchief.) This handkerchief is the world in which he lived. (Pretend to roll the match, but, instead, palm it, and let helper feel the match hidden in the hem. Take the dime from pocket and roll it into the handkerchief.) He had much money, so that he could buy anything he wanted. (Then the bread.) He never was hungry, for he had plenty to eat. (Then the cloth.) He had the finest clothes to wear. (Next the wood.) We build houses of wood. This man had a large and beautiful house. (Finally the grain.) And he had large fields, in which grew corn and wheat. While he had more than enough for himself, there were poor people who were hungry. But this did not bother him.

This man had everything he wanted, but he could not take anything with him into the next world. One night he died and he was gone. Oh, yes, we said that the match in the handkerchief was the rich man. Let us see what happened to the match. (Unroll handkerchief.) The match is gone, but the dime (hold each article up separately), the bread, the cloth, the wood, and the grain are still here. So the rich man, when he left to go to the other world, had to leave his money, his food, his fine clothes, his beautiful house, and all his grain. He was gone, but these were all here. He could not take any of them with him. What we can take along with us into the next world are the good things that we can put into our hearts and souls, such as love, kindness, good deeds, and beautiful thoughts.

18

THE LIGHT THAT WOULD NOT GO OUT

Materials:

A tall tumbler.

A deep glass mixing bowl or a fish bowl.

A square of thin board a little larger than the open end of the tumbler.

A very small candle, preferably a birthday candle.

Demonstration:

Fill the glass bowl with water nearly to the top. Fasten the candle directly in the center of the square of wood and set it afloat in the bowl of water. Light the candle. Invert the tumbler over the lighted candle and push the square of wood down until the candle is actually burning beneath the surface of the water. The air in the glass prevents the water entering it. The audience can see the candle burn beneath the water. The flame will soon consume the air in the glass, and the candle should be brought to the surface and the glass removed before the flame is extinguished by a lack of air. If the glass is removed too quickly, the inrushing air will extinguish the flame. To assure success a little experimenting is required.

Story:

Jesus said: " I am the light of the world." It may seem strange that Jesus should say that He was a light. Just what did He mean by this?

For what do we use a light? We need a light when it is dark, so that we can see. The world was very dark when Jesus came into it. I do not mean the kind of darkness we have at night. The darkness Jesus spoke of was sin, godlessness, hate, murder, stealing, lying, and cruelty. The people needed some one to lead them out of this darkness. What is needed in such a darkness is a light, so that people can follow it. God sent Jesus to be such a light. And when He came, He said, " I am the light of the world." But the Bible tells us that the people preferred darkness to the light. And so they killed Jesus, thinking that in that way they could put out the light that He was.

Ordinarily, when we put a light under water it goes out. (Set lighted candle afloat in the bowl of water.) This candle represents Jesus, the light. (Submerge it.) They put Jesus to death, but not His light. (Bring lighted candle to surface.) Jesus became a light in twelve men who became His disciples. Shortly before Jesus left this earth, He told these twelve disciples that they, too, were lights and that they should never allow their lights to go out. As they went from place to place they preached the things that Jesus had taught them. But many people did not like this, for it meant that they would have to give up many things that were wrong. They did not want to do this. So they put the disciples in jail or killed them. One would think that the light Jesus had given them would have gone out. (Submerge lighted candle.) But it did not.

A later disciple was Paul. Jesus, who had now left this earth, appeared to Paul one day. From that day on, Jesus became a light in him. He went to distant places, preaching about Jesus and telling every one that there would be no darkness in the world and that every one would be happy if he did as Jesus told him. They took this Paul to the big city of Rome, put him in prison, and then beheaded him. They tried to put out his light. (Submerge candle.) But it would not go out.

Paul had made many new Christians in many places. And each one of these became a light. They had in them the light of Jesus. These Christians refused to obey the emperor when they were told not to worship Christ. Many of these Christians were killed; their heads were cut off, and many were thrown to the lions. They tried to put out the light of Jesus in them. (Submerge candle.) But it would not go out.

These Christians gave the light of Jesus to others, and that is how we got the Christian Church. Good and true Christians around the whole world have the light of Jesus in them. This light must not be allowed to go out. If it does, the world will be in darkness. If we love Christ and follow Him we have His light in us. (Submerge candle.) Do not let this light go out.

19

THE GREATEST GIFT WE CAN GIVE

Materials:

Three envelopes.

Demonstration:

Paste two of the envelopes back to back. This will give the appearance of one envelope. On four slips of paper write these four questions:

1. What is the greatest gift we can give to God?
2. How much did God love the world?
3. Where is God?
4. What did Jesus say about little children?

Read them aloud and deposit them in the side of the double envelope toward the audience. In the side of the double envelope toward you, you have beforehand put four slips of paper, and on each one is written the same question, " What is the greatest gift we can give to God? " In the third envelope lying on the table you have beforehand placed a slip of paper containing the answer to this question. The answer is: " The greatest gift we can give to God is ourselves." Then, when you ask some one to draw out one of the four slips in the double envelope, you turn that side of the double envelope toward him which contains the four slips, each of which has the same question on it. The one who does the drawing thinks he has a choice of four questions, when, in reality, he draws the same question, no matter which slip he chooses. Have your helper read the question on the slip he has drawn. Then instruct him to find the answer in the third envelope on the table. This envelope, containing only one slip, has the correct answer to the question he drew. Ask him to make certain that there are no other slips in it. It appears miraculous that the one slip in the envelope on the table should contain the correct answer to the particular question which he drew, when, apparently, he had a choice of four questions.

Story:

(Perform the trick.) We have found the correct answer to our question. What is the greatest gift we can give to God? (Have your helper read the answer again.) That is it. We can make God happy by giving ourselves to Him.

How can boys and girls give themselves to God? Let us try to answer that question in this way. Your fathers and mothers love you very much. Now, what can you do to make them happy? You say, " I will give them a present with the money I have saved." And if you did that I am sure they would say " Thank you," and they would be pleased. But you would make them much happier if you said to them, " I love you very much." By saying that you give yourself to your father and mother. Now, the present you give them is, no doubt, very nice, but the best present you can give them is yourself. They want you much more than they want your present.

As your father and mother want you, in the same way God wants you. And you make God very happy when you give yourself to Him. On Sundays you bring some money to church. You are giving that money to God. God is pleased with that. You should give this money. But God can be made happiest when you give yourself to Him. How can you give yourself to God? By being His boy or girl, by loving Him, by listening to what He whispers in your ear, by doing what you know pleases Him, by worshipping Him, by praying to Him. When we do this, then we have given ourselves to God.

I read a story which will help you to understand what it means to give ourselves, and I want you to hear it. So listen.

" Once upon a time there was a fair young maiden who had five brothers. One was a musician, the second was a painter, the third was a merchant, the fourth was a cook, and the fifth was a builder.

" Now, this fair young maiden had a beautiful diamond which her father had given her, and each of the brothers wanted it for himself.

" The first who sought it was the musician. He came

to her and said, 'Sell it to me; I will play you some beautiful music for it.' But she said, 'And when the music is ended I should have nothing'; and she refused to sell her diamond for music.

"Then came the painter. 'I will paint you a splendid picture for your diamond,' he said. But she replied, 'Your splendid picture might be stolen or its color might fade. I will not sell my diamond to you.'

"Next came the merchant. 'O sister,' he said, 'I will bring you such spices and perfumes from the East in my ships as you never smelled the like of; and I will give you sweet-smelling roses and lilies, a garden full.' But she said, 'The perfumes will cease to please me, and the roses and lilies will fade.'

"Then the cook came and said, 'Dear sister, I will prepare for you a splendid banquet of the finest, richest things you could eat; give your diamond to me.' But she said, 'After the banquet I should be hungry again and my diamond gone; no, I will not sell it to you.'

"Then the builder came. He offered to build her a beautiful palace to live in—a palace that might do for a queen. 'But a palace is filled with cares, even to its queen,' she said, 'and I cannot sell my diamond for a house full of cares.'

"At last, when all the brothers had been refused, came the prince of a great kingdom and said he wished to buy the diamond. 'And what will you give me for my diamond?' she asked. 'I will give myself,' he said, 'myself, and all I possess.' Hearing that, the young maiden answered, 'I accept that gift. I will be yours and you shall be mine forever.' Whereupon she gave him the diamond."

The prince said, "I will give myself and all I possess." That is what we should say to God. And when we do that we will belong to God, and God will belong to us. The greatest gift we can give to God is ourselves.

20

TRUE FRIENDSHIP

Materials:

A string or tape about eighteen inches long.

Demonstration:

Lay the tape across the upturned palms of your hands placed side by side with the little fingers of both hands next to each other. Let the ends hang down between the thumb and index finger of each hand. Then bring your palms together quickly, at the same time secretly catching hold of the middle of the tape with the fourth and fifth fingers. With the tape in this position ask your helper to tie your thumbs together tightly. While it appears as if he were tying them tightly, in reality he is not, because you hold the tape between your palms. After the thumbs are tied, have the helper place a hat over your hands. Blow on the hat for effect, while you slip your thumbs from under the tape. When the hat is removed, the thumbs are free. When the hat is replaced over your hands by the helper, blow on the hat again, and slip your thumbs under the tape. When the hat is removed, your thumbs will appear tied as at first.

Story:

The one person for whom we should feel more sorry than any other is the one who has no friends. I cannot imagine anyone who has no friends at all. Sometimes, when everything seems to go wrong, we hear some one say: " I haven't a friend in the world." If we have no friends the trouble is not with others; the fault is with us. If we go out of our way to be friendly, then we will have friends. The one who has many friends first of all has been a friend to others. We all need friends; we cannot live without them.

True friendship between two people is very beautiful. One of the finest examples of friendship is that of Jonathan and David in the Bible. Jonathan was the son of a rich king, and David was only a poor shepherd. The people wanted David as their next king. One would think that this should have made Jonathan very jealous, because he, as the king's son, should have been the next king. But Jonathan did everything to help David become the next king. Of this beautiful friendship the Bible says: " The soul of Jonathan was knit with the soul of David, and Jonathan loved him as his own soul."

Look at that word " knit." To knit means to tie together. (Have helper tie thumbs.) As these two thumbs are tied together with a tape, so Jonathan and David were tied together with love for one another. (Have hat placed over hand.) Sometimes friendships are broken like this. (Show thumbs untied.) We must be careful not to break the ties that bind us to our friends. (Replace hat over hands and slip thumbs under tape.) We must be knit or tied to our friends like this. (Reveal tied thumbs.) Good friends are worth more than gold and silver.

I will tell you another story of two friends who were tied together by love as these two thumbs are tied together. Pythias was condemned to die by Dionysius, the king. But before he died, Pythias wanted to go home to take care of some things. Dionysius would allow him to go only on condition that Pythias' friend Damon should take his place in prison. Should Pythias not return at a fixed time, then Damon would have to die in his place. So Damon took Pythias' place in prison while Pythias went home. Pythias was delayed. He did not come, and still he did not come. Finally, Dionysius would wait no longer for his return, and he had Damon led out of prison to be executed. But Damon still believed that Pythias would return. Just as he was about to be killed, Pythias suddenly rushed through the crowd into the arms of his friend Damon. When Dionysius saw this beautiful friendship between these two, he set both Damon and Pythias free, and asked if he, too, could be their friend.

Indeed, besides being a friend of God's there is nothing more beautiful than to be a friend of others.

21

THE LOVE OF MOTHERS
(MOTHER'S DAY)

Materials:

A tumbler made of clear glass.
A sheet of typewriter paper.

Demonstration:

Lay the sheet of typewriter paper on a table or chair. With a red crayon write on the center of the sheet the two words, " Mother's Love." Paste a piece of paper of the same kind over the open end of the tumbler and trim the edges very closely. Place the tumbler upside down on one end of the sheet, and it will not be noticed that the open end is covered. Throw a handkerchief over it and set it directly over the two words. Remove the handkerchief, and the false paper over the open end of the tumbler conceals the two words. Reverse the process and the words will reappear.

Story:

All of us either have a mother or have had one. So Mother's Day is something that all of us can celebrate. Mother should be remembered. If she is no longer with us but has gone on into the other world, we should honor her by thinking of her often. If you still have a mother you should be happy and show your love. We should do this because mothers love their children.

Mother's love is more like the love of God than anything we know. God loves all people, even if they are bad and wicked. Jesus told us about the Prodigal Son who left home, spent his father's money, and lived a bad life. And when his friends left him and he was hungry and his clothes were in rags, he went back home. Did the father close the door against him or did he take him in? The father was glad to see him. Jesus said that God loves us as that father loved his son. And the love of a good mother is like the love of God.

Some people become criminals. They steal, kill, or do some such terrible thing. Some of these criminals have good mothers, and they love them even if they are bad. I will tell you about one such mother.

Once a year in France the worst criminals are put in a ship and taken to a lonely island in the sea. They will never come back; they stay there as long as they live. It means that they will be separated forever from father, mother, sisters, and brothers.

Once a mother whose son was a criminal, and who was to be shipped to that lonely island, hid herself on the boat. The next day, when all the criminals marched into the ship, she rushed out from her hiding place and threw her arms around her son's neck and with tears streaming down her cheeks, gave him a last kiss. The soldiers as quickly as possible rushed the mother off the boat. But, at least, that mother had done all she could; she still loved her son even though he was a criminal. Mother was the very best friend that man had. When every one deserted him, she remained true to him; when every one doubted him, she still believed in him. Her love for her son never changed.

Good mothers are like that. Doubtless that mother corrected her son when he was as young as you are, if he did something that was wrong. She warned him; perhaps she sent him to bed without his dinner; perhaps she took away his privileges or his weekly allowance. When she corrected him, he very likely thought that she no longer loved him. (Place tumbler covered with handkerchief over the words, " Mother's Love.") Look, the words, " Mother's Love," have disappeared. Can the love of a good mother for her child disappear like that? No, never! That mother's love followed her criminal son on board that ship and to that lonely island as long as she lived. (Cover tumbler and remove it, and the words have miraculously reappeared.) " Mother's Love " is still here. When mothers at times have to punish their children for wrongs they have done, it is not because they do not love them. They do this because they do love them. Let us thank God for our mothers.

22

THE LITTLE GIANTS

Materials:

Two sharp knives.

A piece of soft wood about two feet long.

A piece of hard wood or an iron rod.

Two strips of paper, about two inches wide and twelve inches long, with the ends pasted together, forming a ring or a loop.

Demonstration:

Two helpers are necessary; have them stand about three feet apart facing each other and holding the knives extended. Place the paper rings, one on the blade of each knife. Then take your two-foot piece of soft wood and suspend it through the lower ends of the paper rings. Stand a short distance away with the rod in your right hand and strike the piece of soft wood a sharp blow in the center and it will break in half.

Story:

It has often been said, " The pen is mightier than the sword." Do you believe that?

The mouse sometimes is stronger than the lion. Do you think that is true? Well, let us listen to Æsop's fable of the *Lion and the Mouse.*

Once upon a time when a lion was fast asleep, a little mouse began running up and down and over him. This soon wakened the lion, who roared as he put his paw on the mouse and said, " I am going to eat you." " Oh, King Lion," squeaked the little mouse, " please, forgive me this time. Who knows, maybe I'll be able to help you sometime? " The lion was so amused at the idea of a little mouse helping him that he lifted up his paw and allowed the little mouse to run away.

Shortly after this, King Lion was caught in a trap, a sort of a net. He filled the whole forest with his roars. The little mouse heard the commotion and ran as fast as she could to see what was wrong. And, lo, she saw that the lion was caught in a net. So she went up to the lion and said, " Be quiet, King Lion, and I will help you." So she started to gnaw the ropes of the net trap, until, finally, she had gnawed them completely through. The king of beasts was free once more. " See, King Lion," said the little mouse, " was I not right? Even if I am little, I was able to help a great king like you."

Was I right? Do you think this little mouse was stronger than the lion?

Now I need two helpers. George and Frank, will you help me? (Perform trick.) What do you think of this, the weak paper proved to be stronger than a piece of wood? Did you think that this paper, which can easily be torn into shreds without the least effort, could withstand a hard blow with this iron rod on this piece of wood?

Jane was a little girl in the Beginners Department in Sunday school. Her mother and father never came to church. After Jane had been in Sunday school about six months, there was to be a special children's service in the church. Jane persuaded her parents to attend. After this, every Sunday morning, Jane would say, " Daddy and mother, come to God's house with me today, won't you? " So gradually Jane won daddy and mother over to God's side.

You see, the little, weak mouse helped the big, strong

lion. Small, wee Jane helped her big, strong parents.
Doesn't this remind us of the words of Jesus which we
can all follow, " A little child shall lead them "? Even
if we are small and weak we can be strong, can we not?

There is a text in the Bible which says, "And God
chose the weak things of the world, that he might put
to shame the things that are strong."

23

YIELD NOT TO TEMPTATION

Materials:

A tumbler.

A hard-boiled egg.

An eight- or nine-inch tin or aluminum pie plate.

A cylinder four inches high and an inch and a half
in diameter, made of corrugated cardboard.

An ordinary straw house broom.

Demonstration:

Set the tumbler, half full of water, about two inches
from the edge of the table. Place the pie plate with the
flange up exactly over the center of the tumbler. The
pie plate in this position should extend about an inch
over the edge of the table. Then place the cylinder
exactly on the center of the pie plate, and on top of
the cylinder put the egg with the pointed end upward.
The audience need not know that the egg is boiled. An
unboiled egg may be used just as well. The object is
to drop the egg into the tumbler of water without
removing the pie plate with your hands and without

touching the egg. To do this place your foot firmly on the straw of the broom, and when the handle is perpendicular to the floor, it should be about three inches away from the edge of the table, aimed directly at the center of the pie plate. With your foot firmly on the straw, draw the handle back about six inches from the table and then let it fly directly at the pie plate. The pie plate and cylinder will fly from under the egg, and the egg will drop into the water. The apparently impossible has been done. The accomplishment of this trick is much easier than it appears to be.

Story:

When people are honest, true, loyal, and faithful they live a good life. Some of these good people are very certain of themselves; they walk erect with their heads held high. They boast that they are strong and nothing can make them a thief, a liar, or a drunkard. All such people who are so sure of themselves should be very careful. The apostle Paul said, " Let him who thinks that he stands be careful that he does not fall." Did you ever see a man go down the street on an icy day with a firm and steady walk, and then all at once step on some ice and go down? He thought he could not fall, but he did. The ice was like a trap; he fell on it, was caught and hurt himself.

Hunters go out to trap wild animals. Did those animals think that anyone could ever trap them? Of course not. How does the hunter trap them? He puts a piece of food in the trap which the animal likes very much. And then when the animal takes the food, the trap is sprung and he is caught. To catch a mouse you put a piece of cheese in the trap. The mouse is certain that he will not be caught; if he thought there

was any danger of getting caught, he would stay far
enough away from the cheese.

There is a poem by Mary Howitt of a spider and a
fly. The spider invited the fly to come into her parlor
in order to trap the fly in her web. But the fly did not
want to come in. Then the spider promised the fly the
best food if only she would come in. But still the fly
refused. Finally the spider told the fly how beautiful
she was, that she had wings like silver and pearl, and
eyes like diamonds. With all this flattery, the vain fly
at last came near enough so that the spider could spring
the trap and she was caught. Then the spider ate the
fly.

As animals and flies get caught, so people, too, are
caught in a trap. This glass with water in it is a trap.
This pie plate we will set over the top of this trap to
make certain that no one will fall into this trap. This
egg is some boy or girl, or some man or woman. There
is no danger now of the egg falling into the trap. (Set
the egg on the pie plate.) And to make doubly certain
that the egg will not get into the trap we will place it
far enough away. (Place cylinder on plate and egg on
top of cylinder.) Now the egg is perfectly safe; it
cannot get into the trap below. But is it safe? Let us
not be too sure.

Sometimes you are tempted to tell a lie. Be careful.
This lie is like the cheese on the mouse trap; the lie will
lead you into a trap. God said, " Thou shalt not lie."

Sometimes people are tempted to steal; some will
even steal money from a bank. Be careful. Stealing
is like all the good things the spider promised the fly.
The fly was caught in the trap. Stealing leads people
into a trap and often into jail. God said, " Thou shalt
not steal."

Sometimes the temptation to do wrong is very strong. Do not boast that no temptation can trap you. When you walk on slippery ice do not boast that you will never fall. This will make you careless and before you know it you will be on your back. Better walk carefully. This egg, we said, is some person. Hear him boast. He says, " I am far away from the trap; I will never be caught; no one will ever knock my feet from under me." And then all at once he comes tumbling down, and is caught in the trap. (Let the broom handle fly against the pie plate.) He was too sure of himself.

The apostle Paul said, "When I am weak then I am strong." By this he meant that he knew he was weak, and when he realized this he called on God for strength and that made him strong. But the person who boasts that he is strong and that he does not need God and that nothing can trap him is in danger. He is likely to get into a trap. God makes us strong; He can keep us out of traps if we ask Him to do so.

24

HAPPINESS AND LOVE

Materials:

Two empty match boxes.
Two marbles; one red, the other green.
Two crayons; one red, the other green.

Demonstration:

Show the empty match boxes and place the red marble in one, and the green marble in the other. Beforehand, the boxes are prepared by marking with crayon the end of the match-box drawers. One is marked red, the other green. These marked ends are kept toward the performer. The red marble is placed in the box which was secretly marked green. So that the spectators may know that the red marble is in this box, the performer puts a red mark on the end of the drawer toward them. Likewise, the green marble is placed in the box which was secretly marked red, and a green mark is put on the end of the drawer toward the audience. The marks put on the boxes before the spectators should be similar to those that were put on secretly. In laying the boxes on the table, they are turned end for end. The performer opens the box which they see is marked green, and to their surprise it contains the red marble. And the box marked red will contain the green marble.

Story:

We all want to be happy. Jesus said that every person ought to be happy and has a right to be happy. He told us that we are living in God's world and that all of us are God's children. This should make us happy. The trouble is that many think that happiness is to be found at some other place than where they are now. And so they go chasing about looking for happiness. In that way we will never find happiness; it only makes us more unhappy. We can be happy right where we are. Happiness is something that is in our hearts.

If the engine in the automobile is not working right, we do not look for the trouble in the tires or the trunk or the cushions on the seat. We must look for the trouble in the engine, for that is where the trouble is.

If we are unhappy, grouchy, and cranky, or if we

think that every one else is to blame for everything we do not like, we may be certain that the trouble is with ourselves. Boys and girls sometimes think that other people make them unhappy. As a rule other people do not make us unhappy; usually we make ourselves unhappy. If that is so, then there must be a change within us.

(At this point in the story perform trick.) There has been a complete change. The red marble is in the box marked green, and the green marble is in the box marked red. The marbles moved into the other boxes. We can move into a new world if we will change our hearts. How can this be done?

There is a story told by Zelia M. Walters * about a girl named Greta who was unhappy because of the kind of people who lived near her. One day Greta went to a little old lady who lived in a small cottage far up the mountain side. Because she was very wise many people came to her when they were in trouble. Greta told this little old godmother what terrible neighbors she had, and that she wanted to move into a new neighborhood where the people were better. The godmother promised her that with her magic powers she could move her into a new neighborhood. The godmother warned Greta that in that new pleasant neighborhood she would have to be kind and courteous so that the other children would like her. Greta promised to do this. Then the old lady gave her a pair of magic glasses that would move her into the new neighborhood.

So Greta put on the glasses and started home. They surely were magic. The world looked so much more beautiful through them. She saw flowers which she had

---

* *The Magic Glasses*, copyrighted by the American Baptist Publication Society. Used by permission.

not seen before. The mountains were fairer than ever.
All the people she met were happy. She joined whole-
heartedly in all their fun. After a whole week in this
pleasant new neighborhood, Greta went back to the old
lady and brought her some roses. She wanted to know
the name of the magic glasses.

The godmother said, " They are named LOVE. You
have been looking out on the world through the magic
of love all this week and you found it a good and happy
world, didn't you? "

" Yes, godmother, very good and happy, but does
that mean that I did not move at all? "

" No, my child. You did move into a different world.
You do see different neighbors. But your house did
not move an inch away from where it stood. But you
yourself moved out of a world of hate into a world of
love."

Since Greta had moved into this new kingdom of
love, her old neighbors who once seemed so terrible now
were good folks. Greta did not need the magic glasses
any longer, she now had the magic in her heart. Remember how the marbles mysteriously moved into the
other boxes. Like Greta, we can move into a happy
world.

25

CHILDREN OF MANY COLORS
(CHILDREN'S DAY)

Materials:

Five crayons, white, black, yellow, red, and brown.

Demonstration:

Put these crayons into an open box on the table directly behind you. Have some one rearrange the crayons in the box behind you to avoid the suspicion that they have been placed in consecutive order. Select a crayon with your hand behind your back and make a small mark on your thumb nail. With your hands still behind you, wrap the crayon in a handkerchief. Bring the wrapped crayon up to your forehead in the hand that has the marked thumb nail, at the same time noting the color of the mark which will identify the crayon selected. The handkerchief against your forehead will give the impression that you are thinking hard to identify the crayon. You name the color and unwrap the crayon for their inspection.

Story:

(Perform demonstration with all five colors.) These five colored crayons represent children whose skins are black, yellow, white, red, and brown. God did not want to make all people white. Do you like to look at pictures that are all white? You boys and girls like pictures that have many colors in them. You like red, black, brown, and all the other lovely colors. God, too, likes many colors and that is why He made some people black, some yellow, some red, some brown, and others white. The white people think that their color is the most beautiful, and the brown people think that their color is the best, and the same, no doubt, is true about the other colored people. But to God one color is as beautiful as the others.

There is a fine story told by Margaret Applegarth * which I want to tell you. The people of a certain community had just built a church. When the people came to see the new church they all thought that it was very

* *How the Artist Forgot Four Colors*, Harper & Brothers, Publishers.

beautiful. But they said, " We need one thing more; we need hanging in the very front of our church where every one can see it, a picture of Jesus blessing the little children." So they went to the greatest artist and asked him to paint such a picture of Jesus with the little children.

The artist worked hard for many days on the picture. At last it was finished. Jesus was in the very center of the picture and around Him were five children. Then the artist wrote a letter to the people telling them that the picture was finished and that tomorrow they could come to see it. He was happy but tired, and went to bed to get rest.

That night he had a dream. He dreamt that he heard some one at the picture. He hurried into the studio, and there he saw a stranger with a brush in his hand painting on the picture. " Stop," said the artist, " you are spoiling my picture." The stranger calmly said, " When I came into the room I saw that you had spoiled it yourself, so I am merely making it right. You had five colors in your paint box. Why did you use only one? Who ever told you that all children Jesus loves have white faces? " " But who are you? " asked the artist. The stranger said, " I am Jesus, who said, ' Suffer the little children to come unto me and forbid them not, for of such is the kingdom of heaven.' " Then He disappeared. The artist looked at the picture and saw that the stranger had painted one child's face yellow (point to the colored crayon in your hand), another brown, another black, and still another red, and the fifth one was white. The artist looked and looked at it, and he liked it more and more. When he awoke, the sun was shining; it was a dream.

He rushed into the studio and the picture was just

as he had left it, with all the faces white. He knew that God had spoken to him in the dream. He took his brush and painted one child's face (point to the colored crayon) yellow, another brown, another black, another red, and the fifth one he left white. Then the people came to look at the picture, and they were well pleased. They hung it in the new church and said to one another, "It is a picture of Jesus with all the little children that belong to the heavenly Father's family."

26

GOD GIVES LIGHT

Materials:

Two white candles, one tall, the other small.

Demonstration:

Light the tall candle. With a taper transfer the flame from the tall candle to the small one. Let the wick on the small candle get well started, then extinguish flame. As the stream of smoke rises, hold the taper which you have lighted from the tall candle about three inches above the wick of the small candle, directly in the stream of smoke. The lighted taper should be held in the stream of smoke quickly after the flame has been extinguished. The flame will run down the smoke and light the candle.

Story:

We are told in the Bible that when God first made the world there was nothing but darkness. To know what it means to have nothing but darkness, just close your eyes for a little while. You do not mind it very much to close your eyes and be in darkness, because you know you can open your eyes again and see beautiful light all around you. God did not like the darkness that first covered the whole world. So He did a wonderful thing. As God was moving through the darkness, He said, " Let there be light." Then there was light everywhere. " And God saw the light that it was good."

God set the sun in the sky to give us light in the daytime, and the moon and the stars are lights at night. There would be no light in the sun if God had not put it there; the stars could not shine if they had not first of all received their light from God. All the light in this world comes from God.

But God also made man. He placed a light right in his heart. The Bible tells us that " God created man in his own image." All light comes from God, and when He created man in His image that means that He put a light in man. (Point to the tall white candle which should be lighted before beginning story.) That candle we will say is the light of God. (Point to small white candle.) This little candle is man. You will notice that it is unlit. (With a taper transfer light from tall candle to the small one.) What I did now is like what God did. He transferred His light to man. He made man in His own image. And so man also had a light.

But man did not take very good care of the light that God gave him. One day two brothers, Cain and Abel, were in the field and Cain became very angry and killed his brother Abel. (Blow out small candle.) So the light that God had given to Cain went out. (Point to the smoke rising from candle.) Instead of light there was nothing but black smoke rising to heaven. Cain's wickedness, like this smoke, was rising up to God. Cain's light had gone out.

Many years later there lived a man whose name was David. He was a king. To him God also gave His light just as He gives it to every one else. (Transfer light to small candle.) But David did not take very good care of his light, he committed a very wicked deed. He wanted a certain man out of his way, and so he sent him into a battle where the fighting was the heaviest, knowing that he would be killed there. And so David's light went out. (Blow out small candle.) And, like the smoke from this candle, his sin and wickedness rose up to God. But David was very sorry for what he had done. He asked God to forgive him. (Relight candle; blow it out, and immediately hold lighted taper about three inches over the candle, and the flame will leap down the stream of smoke to the wick.) Did you see the flame run down the stream of smoke to light the candle? When David asked God to forgive him, God's light came down from above right down through the smoke of his sin and wickedness, and brought light into his heart again.

God has given each one of us a light. When we do something that is not right or true, the light is in danger of going out. (Blow at candle enough to rock the flame.) See the flame shake and rock. When we tell a lie it rocks the light that God has put in us. In some people the light has entirely gone out. (Blow out flame.) But when anyone is sorry and asks God to forgive him, God puts a new light in his heart. (Demonstrate by extinguishing flame and let light from taper run down the stream of smoke.) Did you notice how the light comes down from above and runs down? All light comes down from above from God, and comes down to us.

27

OUR TROUBLES AND GOD

Materials:

A glass pie plate.

A cup of water. (Water might be colored to make it visible.)

A small candle. (A large candle cut into a short length.)

A narrow-necked glass or wide-necked bottle.

Demonstration:

Set the candle, lit, into the pie plate of water. Put the glass over the candle. As the flame of the candle goes out, the water rises in the glass.

Story:

Once upon a time, many years ago in Old Testament times, there lived a man named Jonah. God wished him to go to a city called Nineveh to preach to the people there. But Jonah did not want to go; it was too much trouble, he thought.

So he decided to run away from God so that he would have no more trouble. Then he went to a city called Tarshish and went on board a ship to sail away from God and all his troubles. But what do you suppose happened? A great storm arose. Jonah's fellow passengers decided that he was the cause of the storm and they threw him overboard into the ocean. Now he was in more trouble than ever, because he had run away from God. Jonah was very foolish in believing that he could run away from God. God is everywhere, and there is no place where God is not. God can help us in our trouble no matter where we are.

We all have troubles at some time. Boys and girls have troubles. Sometimes they are sick and cannot play; sometimes they do not like their breakfast (oatmeal or cornmeal mush); sometimes they get hurt, fall down and skin their knees; often they cannot get their lessons, etc. Everything seems to go wrong.

What shall we do? Shall we go to God with our troubles and tell Him about them, or shall we run away and try to hide, as Jonah did? If we do as Jonah did, we will only get into more trouble.

Will every one of you watch me? First, I am going to pour this cup of water into this pie plate. I have colored the water in order that you might be able to see it better. Now I will light the candle and set it in the pie plate. We will say that the water represents trouble, shall we? The candle is the boy or girl. So, you see (pointing to the candle), the child is standing in the midst of trouble. (Point to water.) In this trouble we must not try to hide from God as Jonah did. If we do, what will happen? (Put the glass over the candle; as the candle goes out, the water rises in the glass.) Jonah ran away from God, and he was cast into a sea of trouble. You remember, the candle represented the boy or girl. The child ran away from God and the water, which we said represented trouble, rises higher around his neck and finally overwhelms him.

We are not going to hide from God, are we? For we want to be near Him so that He will be a help to us in time of trouble.

28

OUR FLAG AND OUR COUNTRY

Materials:

An American flag made of China silk.   (If a silk flag
is not available, draw and color a flag on a white paper
napkin.)

Three strips of China silk of red, white, and blue.
(As a substitute use a white paper napkin cut into three
strips and colored with crayon.)

Demonstration:

In your right hand hold the red, white, and blue
strips, spreading them enough so that each one is visible.   The flag is crumpled in your right fist and is not
visible because it is hidden behind the three strips.
Now crumple the three strips into your left fist and at
the same time spread out the flag and conceal the three
strips in your left fist and behind the flag.   To all appearances the three separate colors have been united
to make our flag.

Story:

I hold in my hand three strips of cloth.   One is red,
the other white, and the third is blue.   These are also
the colors of our flag, the flag of the United States.
The red stands for courage and sacrifice, the white for
purity and peace, and the blue for loyalty.

Why don't we have a flag of just one color?   Because
one color is not enough.   We said red stands for courage and sacrifice.   We like to see courage in people,

people who are not afraid. George Washington and his soldiers fought hard to make our country free. They spent one cold winter in Valley Forge, where many of the soldiers became sick and many died. But the others held out against the enemy. They had courage and made great sacrifices. But just courage and sacrifice are not enough.

The white stands for purity and peace. When a piece of cloth becomes dirty and soiled, we wash it and it becomes clean and white. Americans should be clean and white at heart. Jesus said, " Blessed are the pure in heart: for they shall see God." White stands also for peace. There should be no war at all. God said, " Thou shalt not kill." We Americans should always work for peace. But purity and peace are not enough.

The blue stands for loyalty. In this country we have our homes. On the soil of the United States grows the food that we eat. Our country gives us shelter and protection. It provides for our education. Here we are free to worship God as we think best. God has blessed our country. We should be loyal to it. Blue stands for loyalty, but that alone is not enough.

A flag all red is not what we want (point to each colored strip respectively), nor one that is all white, nor one that is all blue. We have all three colors in our flag. (Perform the trick.) There is the flag of the United States: red for courage and sacrifice, white for purity and peace, and blue for loyalty. We need all of these qualities to be good Americans.

The forty-eight white stars in one corner of our flag represent the forty-eight states that make up our country. Each star represents a state. Why do we have stars in our flag? Why not something else? Only God can make stars. God holds the stars together in the heavens. God is holding our forty-eight states together, and all together they make one strong nation.

These stars and stripes stand for our country, which we love. But we must love our country in the right way. We love our country, but this does not mean that we should hate other nations. We should love God and our country. And when we love God we cannot hate other nations. We love and respect our flag. Let us also respect the flags of other nations.

29

OUR MONEY

Materials:

Two pennies.

Demonstration:

With a little soap, secretly stick one penny under the edge of the table. Hold the other penny in your hand and assure the audience that you do not have another penny hidden up your sleeve or between your fingers. Lay the penny on the table and rub it back and forth, and then sweep it into your left hand which has been placed at the edge of the table to receive it. Rub the penny between your palms and then throw it upon the table. Make a few unsuccessful attempts. When you are ready to produce the two pennies, loosen the concealed penny with the finger tips of your left hand which is under the edge of the table to receive the penny that is on the table. Rub them between your palms and throw both on the table. Apparently you have made two pennies out of one.

Story:

I hold in my hand a penny. It is the smallest piece of money which we have. But a hundred pennies will make a dollar. We cannot eat pennies and dollars. But we need them to buy food, clothes, houses, and so many other things that make life pleasant and happy. We cannot get along without money. However, there are many other things that are much more important than money. We must not love money more than God or our family and friends. We should love trees, flowers, grass, and sunshine more than money. Jesus told us of a certain rich man who piled up more and more dollars. And, finally, when he was very rich, he said to himself, " Now I can take it easy." But that night God said to him, " Tonight you will lose your soul." And during the night he died. If he had loved God, friends, flowers, and trees more than his money he would not have lost his soul.

But, as I said before, we need money. Let us use money as a carpenter uses his hammer, or as a gardener uses his spade. God wants us to earn more money. That is why Jesus told about three men, each of whom was given a certain amount of money. The first two took their money and went out to earn more money with it. These two thought that if they could earn more money they would have enough for themselves, and the rest they could use to help others. But the third man buried his money and did not earn more money with it. He was a lazy man. Jesus told us to be like the first two men, who went out to earn money, and not like the third man. We can do much good with our money if we use it right.

Here is a penny. (Show penny.) We cannot make money by magic; we have to work for it. But a ma-

gician can do queer tricks. Let us try to make two
pennies out of one. (Perform trick.) We have two
pennies where before we had only one. You cannot
make money this way by magic, but we can all earn
money by working for it. I merely showed you this
trick to impress upon you that by work you can have
two pennies where before you had only one.

By work we can get many other things that make our
lives happier and more beautiful. We must work for
money. We must work to learn to play the piano. We
must work in school to improve our minds. We must
work at home to make it easier for others. We must
work in the church to help others to be more religious
and to think more of God. Money is only one of the
many things for which we work. And of all the things
for which we work, money, perhaps, is the least important. It certainly is the least important to God.
But we need money also, and God wants us to work
for it.

30

THE CREATION

Materials:

A glass pie plate filled with water.

A piece of sodium, the size of a peppercorn. (This
may be obtained at a shop where chemicals are sold or
at the high-school or college chemical department.)

Demonstration:

Set the glass pie plate filled with water in a conspicu-
ous place, so that your entire audience may be able to
see it. Drop into it the piece of sodium. (Be careful

that the piece is no larger than specified.) The sodium will burst into flame and smoke and will dart from one side of the plate to the other.

Story:

Our story today is based on a text from the Bible. It is found in Genesis, the first book of the Bible, in the first chapter and the second verse: " And the Spirit of God moved upon the face of the waters."

Thousands of years ago the world was not as it is today. The Bible tells us that it was " waste and void and the Spirit of God moved upon the face of the waters." In the beginning there was no life. Only God was here. (Show trick.) God moved over the waste just as this sodium moved over the waters but God brought forth life. With God there was life, just as there is life in the sodium. When God moved over the waste, things began to happen.

There was no day; there was no night. But God said, " Let there be light and there was light." But still the world was a dreary place, with no people, no animals, nor even a blade of green grass.

But God looked down upon this waste and void and thought " I will change all this." So He divided the water and the ground. But still the world did not look beautiful, so God caused trees, bushes, and flowers to grow. How beautiful His world was becoming.

But He wished it to be still more delightful, so He brought animals to move about in the growing vegetation and sweet singing birds to fly around in the tree tops.

Still, there seemed to be one thing lacking. Oh, yes, there were no people to enjoy this wonderful world. So God took some dust of the ground and from it He

made a man. He breathed the breath of life into him
and he became a living soul.

Then God looked upon all that He had made, and,
behold, it was good. "And the Spirit of God moved
upon the face of the waters."

31

OVERCOMING DIFFICULTIES

Materials:
   A tumbler.
   A candle.

Demonstration:

The performer lights the candle, places it on the table, and then puts the tumbler between the candle and
himself. He then blows against the glass and the candle
is extinguished, the air having apparently passed right
through the glass. In reality, if you blow against the
center of the glass the air currents divide and reunite
on the opposite side of the glass, striking the flame with
all their original strength.

Story:

   " Somebody said that it couldn't be done,
      But he, with a chuckle, replied
      That maybe it couldn't, but he would be one
      Who wouldn't say ' no ' till he tried." *

* " It Couldn't Be Done," by Edgar A. Guest, from the book, *The
Path to Home,* copyright 1919. Used by permission of The Reilly &
Lee Co., Chicago, Ill.

The wise man Epictetus said, " Difficulties are things that show what men are."

Many, many years ago, hundreds of years before Christ was born, the people of Israel were trying to conquer the entire country of Palestine. The name of their king was Saul, and they were fighting against the Philistines, a tall, war-like people.

One day, just before a battle, a big, tall Philistine, a giant named Goliath, came strutting before the army of Saul, calling, " Whoever will come out here, fight and conquer me, will win the war, but if I win, we Philistines will be victorious."

None of Saul's soldiers volunteered; they were all afraid, saying that they would never, never be able to conquer so big a man. A shepherd boy named David heard that challenge. He went to King Saul and said, " I will fight Goliath." Every one tried to dissuade him, for he was only a boy, but David said, " I go with the help of God." He chose some smooth stones and with these and his slingshot he went to meet the giant, and, would you believe it, with one little round stone thrown with the slingshot he killed the mighty Goliath.

Was David the only one to overcome difficulties? Edison was deaf, but he was a great inventor. Robert Louis Stevenson was continually ill, but he became a great author. And we could name many more.

What about you? Is your giant Laziness? Can you overcome him? Is your difficulty a sharp tongue? Can you bridle that? Now, let us see what we can do about that.

Let us say that the candle represents a goal, something we would like to be or attain. We will set the glass between the candle and us. Shall we call the glass Laziness? Do you think that we can overcome

Laziness? Do you think that we will be able to blow out the candle? Shall we try? What has happened to the candle? Yes, it has been extinguished.

It seemed impossible to blow out the candle on the other side of the glass but we did it, did we not? It often seems impossible to do right, to obey and perform certain duties, but if we try, we can overcome all of these difficulties, just as I was able to extinguish this candle.

32

THE EASY WAY

Materials:

Soup plate.
A tumbler.
A penny.
Some water discolored with ink.
Some dry paper.
A match.

Demonstration:

Pour enough of the discolored water into the soup plate to cover the bottom of the plate. Near the edge or rim of the plate drop the penny into the water. The problem is how to get the penny out of the dirty water without staining your fingers. The dish must not be moved, nor the penny handled with any instrument, nor the water ladled off with a spoon. Stuff a little dry paper into the tumbler and light it. When the paper is blazing, set the tumbler upside down in the water. The water will be sucked up into the tumbler, leaving the penny dry. Remove the penny before the water falls back.

Story:

There is always an easy way to do everything, and there is also a hard way. Sometimes the easy way is just as good and better than the hard way. For example, if I want to cross the ocean, it is easier to take a ship across than to swim across. It is not only easier, it is safer. But very often the easy way is not the best way. There is no easy way to get an education. The way to get it is to go to school, study, read, and work hard. There are some boys and girls who are not honest, who cheat in an examination. They are doing it the easy way. They are not only not learning anything, but they are hurting themselves. Every time we cheat or are dishonest we have stained our souls.

Now, here is a penny. (Drop it in the discolored water.) How can I get it out of the dirty water? The easy way would be to pick it out with my fingers, but if I do so, my fingers will be stained. The easy way in life often leaves blotches and stains on our souls. (Perform trick.) The harder, more difficult, and longer way was the best way to get the penny out of the dirty water without staining my fingers.

Most people want to be rich. And in order to get more money some will cheat, lie, and steal. This may be an easy way to get money, but it certainly is not the best way. This easy way of making money leaves dirty spots on your soul. The harder way of getting your pennies and dollars by work is the best way.

There is a fable about a donkey which was carrying home a load of salt on his back. In crossing a stream the donkey stumbled and fell into the water. He lay in the water for some time, and when he finally got on his feet again, he discovered that the salt had melted in the water. So he had no load to carry and this made him happy. Some time later this same donkey was carrying home a load of sponges. Remembering how he had lost his load the last time by falling into the water, he purposely fell again. While salt melts in water, sponges do not. The sponges filled up and his load was many times heavier than before. The lazy donkey got into trouble by trying to find an easy way.

To get the penny out of the dirty water the easy way would leave my fingers stained. To pass an examination in school the easy way by cheating leaves your soul stained. To get more money the easy way by dishonesty leaves a dirty blotch on your heart. The easy way often is the hardest way. The lazy donkey thought of making it easy for himself, but, instead, the load became heavier.

The things that are best and most worth having are those for which we work hard. No, the easy way is not always the best. It certainly is not the best when it stains our fingers, and, worst of all, our hearts.

33

THE GREAT TREASURE HUNT

Materials:

Four small match boxes or any small boxes of the same size.

Three marbles, one golden, the other blue, and the third red.

Three more marbles of any color.

Demonstration:

Put the three marbles of any color in one of the boxes

and fasten it to your wrist under the coat sleeve with a rubber band. Place the other three boxes on a table in full view of the audience. Have the golden, blue and red marbles in a paper bag. Take the golden marble, hold it up, and pretend that you are putting it into one of the three boxes. But in reality you return it to the bag when you next take out the blue marble. Pretend to put the blue marble in the same box, but, as before, you return it to the bag as, finally, you take out the red marble. The red marble, too, seemingly goes into the same box but is secretly dropped into the bag as you crumple it, thereby indicating that it is empty. Then dispose of it by putting it into your pocket. The box you hold in your hand is believed by the audience to contain the three marbles, but in reality it is empty. To make it more real, shake the box. The rattling noise comes from the box fastened to the wrist. Set all three boxes on the table. Ask a helper to identify the box with the marbles in it after you have changed their positions and moved them from place to place. Occasionally shake one of them and the rattling noise leads him to believe that he can select the right one. When he points out his selection and the box is opened, of course it will be found empty.

Story:

Most of us have been on a treasure hunt. It is great fun. It is usually played out of doors. Some one hides a treasure, and all the boys and girls try to find it. The treasure may be anything at all, but usually it is something good to eat. To find the treasure you must follow signs which lead you along all kinds of trails and byways. Occasionally you will find slips of paper which tell you where to go next. Sometimes the signs tell you to go in the wrong direction in order to mislead you. But if you follow the right signs and look hard enough, you will finally find the treasure.

Let me tell you about a great hunt in which all people are looking for the treasure. The treasure for which they are seeking is happiness. Happiness is the greatest treasure in the world. The person who has happiness has everything. Where can we find this treasure? Every one is looking for it, and I know that we, too, are searching for it.

(Exhibit golden marble.) Here is a sign. It is a marble with a golden color. Gold means money, and if we had plenty of money we could buy anything we want, and then, perhaps, we would find the happiness for which we are looking. (Pretend to put the marble in the box.)

(Exhibit blue marble.) This blue marble is also a sign which may lead us to the treasure of happiness. Blue is a good color, and ribbon of that color is pinned on the one who wins the first prize. To win first prize and receive the blue ribbon means that the winner is just a little better than the rest. If we could win blue ribbons, that would make us famous. People would crowd around us, and we would be proud of ourselves, and then, perhaps, we would have the happiness which we all want. (Pretend to put the blue marble into the same box.)

(Exhibit red marble.) Perhaps this red marble can lead us to happiness. Red is an exciting color. Red makes our hearts beat a little faster. Red stands for thrills and excitement; chasing about from one place to another, first to a movie, then for a ride, then to a party, never being quiet and alone with ourselves. Perhaps if we have plenty of thrills, we will find happiness. (Pretend to put the red marble into the same box.)

Now, then, I have put the golden marble of wealth, the blue marble of fame, and the red marble of thrills into the same box. (Shake the empty box, and the rattle will assure the audience that it contains the marbles. Place all three boxes on the table, and as you shift their positions, occasionally shake one. Finally, open the box your helper has selected to contain the marbles. To his surprise, it is empty.) The box is empty; the treasure of happiness is not in it. Money, fame, and thrills are false signs that mislead us. Let us not follow these to find happiness.

Money, fame, and thrills are not the road to happiness. But you ask, "Where, then, can we find happiness?" Jesus said, "Thou shalt love the Lord thy God and thy neighbor as thyself." So, you see, we need not leave our own homes to find true happiness. If we are kind to our parents, our brothers and sisters, and all others, we feel a warm glow within us. If by our acts we lend a helping hand, the light of love will shine through our eyes. Therefore, the place to find the treasure of happiness is in our own hearts. The signs to follow are kindness, truth, goodness, and love of God and our fellow men. This is the way to the treasure of happiness.

34

" GOD AND COMPANY "

Materials:

A paper napkin.
A glass of water.

Demonstration:

Tightly twist the paper napkin into the form of a rope and offer it to a helper to pull apart. Unless he is unusually strong, it will be impossible to tear it in half. Moisten your thumb and index finger in the glass of water and take hold of the twisted napkin in the center. Hold it just long enough for the water to soak in, and return it at once to the helper. Now he will be able to tear it with ease.

Story:

I want to tell you a story about Peter which took place when Herod Agrippa was king of Judea. Herod wished to please the Jews in Jerusalem, so he seized one of the apostles, James, and caused the guards to kill him with a sword. This terrible act pleased the priests and rulers, so Herod also caught Peter and had him put into prison, intending to have him put to death at the next Passover Feast.

So Peter was now in prison, with sixteen soldiers guarding the prison, four of whom watched him continually. Peter knew that his death was certain unless he could in some way get out of prison. He must have thought and thought of some means of escape. (At this time hand twisted napkin to helper, telling him to tear it apart.) You see, just as (name of helper) is trying different ways of tearing apart the twisted napkin, so Peter must have tried to think of ways and means of escape. (Take napkin from helper.)

But, in the meantime, we read in the book of Acts, " But prayer was made without ceasing of the church unto God for him." You see, the church people were praying for Peter continually.

On the night before Peter was to die he was sleeping

in the prison, bound with chains, with the soldiers watching him. Remember, the people were praying. The people were asking God's help in setting Peter free. We need help to tear this napkin. (Moisten your fingers and finish the trick.) You see, a little help was all that was needed. Do you think Peter received any help? Let us go on with the story.

Suddenly a bright light shone into Peter's cell, and an angel stood before him. The angel awoke him and said, " Rise up quickly." As Peter stood up, the chains fell from his hands and the angel bade him follow. Peter followed the angel out of the prison and into the city. Then the angel left Peter, and Peter decided to go to the home of John Mark and his mother. At this home many people had met and were praying for Peter. Peter came to the house and knocked at the door. A young woman named Rhoda came to the door and she knew at once that it was Peter. She ran to tell the news to the others, but they would not believe her. But Peter kept on knocking, and when, at last, they opened the door and saw him, how happy they were. Peter then told them how the Lord, because of their prayers, had brought him out of prison. Then he went away to a place where Herod could not find him.

Soon after this Herod died; but Peter, whom he was so anxious to kill, lived many years, preaching and teaching the gospel of Christ.

All that was needed to tear the napkin was a little help, a little water. All that Peter needed was a little help from God, and he received it through prayer. Those who pray are helped by God, and it is also true that praying people are helping God in His work. In this way they form a great company, called " God and Company."

35

TWO IN ONE

Materials:

A single match.

Demonstration:

Exhibit a single match. Show that your hands are empty and that nothing is up your sleeve. Holding the match away from your body, wave your hand through the air and suddenly two matches instead of one will be seen.

This experiment is done by using a single match, which has been carefully split in two halves with a sharp knife or a razor blade. The two halves are put together and shown to the audience as one match. When the hand is waved in the air, the halves are separated and at a short distance it will be impossible to tell that they are not two whole matches.

Story:

Bobby, how many boys are you? One or two? One, you say. Well, I think that you are two boys, a good boy and sometimes a bad boy. Usually you are a good one, but sometimes the bad one comes out and shows himself.

I'd like to tell you a story which I have heard about a man and his pet alligator. They were very fond of one another; they even slept in the same room. One day the man was taking a nap with the alligator on the floor beneath the bed. While asleep, the man hung his arm over the edge of the bed; the alligator loved his

master so much that he began to lick his hand. The
salty perspiration tasted good, and he licked so much
and so hard that he caused the blood to flow. After the
alligator had had a taste of blood, with a snap he bit
off the hand of his master. The alligator was a good
friend to his master, but his wild nature was too strong.
So you see what happened.

(Perform trick.) Do you see this match? It seems
to be but a single one, does it not? But watch! (Wave
hand in air.) Now, see, there are two matches. In
this one match we found two, did we not?

So we have two natures, a good and an evil one.
Which shall we be, good or bad? Shall we tell lies or
the truth? Shall we steal or be honest? Each one of us
has to decide for himself which is the better. I am sure
we all wish our better nature to rule over our evil one.
The bad in us can lead us to all that is wicked and
sinful, and the good in us to all that is beautiful, lovely,
and right, and to God. Shall we all try to live up
to the words of the poet?

> " Do your best, your very best
>   And do it every day;
> Little boys and little girls,
>   That's the wisest way." *

36

SINS THAT SEPARATE

Materials:

A small glass.

A thin card (index card).

---

* " Do Your Best," from *Prose and Poetry for Young People,* pub-
lished by Penn Publishing Company, Philadelphia, Pa.

A plate or a piece of glass.
A plant.

Demonstration:

Fill the glass brimful of water, lay the thin card over it, and on the card press a plate or a piece of glass. Turn it all upside down and you will be able to raise the glass from the plate without losing any water. The weight of air on the outside of the paper is more than the weight of the water in the glass. Then remove the card and allow the water to fall on the plant.

Story:

One day, while Jesus was still living here on earth, a rich young ruler came to visit Him. He wished to ask Jesus a question. So he said, " Jesus, what shall I do to inherit eternal life? " This meant, "What shall I do so that I may some day live with God in heaven? " Jesus answered, " Young man, you know the commandments. Obey them." But the young man answered, " Jesus, I have kept them all ever since I was a boy." Then Jesus said, " I know what is wrong with you. Sell everything that you have and give it to the poor." Then the young man was sad and sorrowful, for his riches were the one thing that he loved more than God.

(Perform the trick.) You see, this little card is the only little thing between the water and the plant; it keeps the water from the plant. Love of money kept the young man from God. All that the young man had to do (take card from glass and allow water to rain on plant) was to remove that one thing. You see, when I removed this card the plant could get the water which it needed.

What is there between you and God? God wants to

give us many blessings. "There shall be showers of blessing." But, first, we must take away everything that keeps us from getting these blessings from God. You ask, "What keeps me from God?" Have you ever told a lie? Have you ever been angry? Did you ever steal, even a cooky? Have you ever disobeyed father or mother? If so, you are like the little card, there is something between you and God. Take it away, try your very best, and you will be obeying Jesus' command to the rich young ruler and many blessings will be yours.

37

WORKING TOGETHER

Materials:

Two pieces of string, one three inches long, the other eighteen inches in length.

Demonstration:

Loop the two pieces of string together with the two ends of the three-inch string to the top, and the two ends of the eighteen-inch string to the bottom, placing your fingers over the loop. Put the short ends into your mouth, and pretend to chew them. In the meantime, separate the short piece from the long piece with your tongue. Retain this short piece in your mouth and remove the long piece. What appeared to be two pieces of string comes from your mouth in one piece.

Story:

The Bible tells us that we are workers together with

God. If we work together we get things done. " Many hands make light work."

There is a fable about an old man whose sons were always quarreling among themselves. They would not work together. The constant quarreling among his sons made the old father very unhappy. He tried to keep peace among them but the sons would not listen.

Finally, he thought of a way to show them how wrong it was to quarrel. He called all his sons around him. He gathered some sticks and tied them in a bundle. Then he asked each of his sons to try to break the bundle of sticks. They all tried very hard but they all failed. Then the father untied the bundle, gave each son one stick and asked him to break it. Of course, this could be done easily.

By this the father showed his sons that a stick alone and by itself can easily be broken, but when they were all held together in a bundle they could not be broken. So the sons learned the lesson that instead of quarreling and one pulling this way and another that way, they should be united and work together. In their quarreling they were not united, they were divided. The bundle of sticks taught them that " united we stand, divided we fall."

(Hold up the two strings with thumb and index finger over the loop.) Here I have two strings. Both of them are rather short. If the two could be united or made into one, they would be much more useful. Each stick by itself was easily broken. Each son of the old father in the fable, alone, could not do much. Each one of these two strings alone is not very useful, but if we could unite them, we would be able to tie up a much bigger package. (Perform trick.) See, we have made one string out of two, without tying a knot in them. The two strings can now work as one. One long string is better than two short ones. Two or three boys and girls working together can do more than each working alone.

But the Bible tells us that we are not only to work together, we are to work together with God. There are so many good things that God wants us to do. We must work with God because without Him we cannot do much. God is always working with us. We could not grow flowers, vegetables, and fruit in our gardens if God did not help us. For this God gives us good ground, He sends the rains and gives sunshine. Without these we could not grow anything. All we have to do is to hoe the garden and keep out the weeds. When we do this we are working together with God.

We are all together here in the church. By worshipping God together and doing together all the good things God wants us to do, we are strong. Let us remember that the sticks in a bundle are stronger than each stick alone. The two strings united into one are more useful than each by itself. We can do the most good and live best if we are united and united in God. We can do together what we cannot do alone. When we all work together for the good of everyone, we are at the same time working together with God.

38

DISCOURAGEMENTS

Materials:

Two candles in holders.

A bit of potassium. (This can be procured in a drug store; also in high-school or college laboratories.)

A little water.

A match.

Demonstration:

With the match light one of the candles. Then dip the other end of this match in the water and transfer a drop of water to the wick of the other candle. This second candle has been prepared by inserting a bit of potassium at the base of the new wick, which has been dampened with coal oil. On contact with the water, the wick will fizz, burst into a flame, and light the candle.

Story:

We all have discouragements and disappointments in our lives at one time or another. When this happens, there are some who want to give up. In the Bible we are told of a prophet named Elijah who was a good and godly man. He was anxious to have all people serve and love God. So wherever he went, he told about God. But most of the people were worshipping an idol called Baal. Then Elijah became so discouraged that he wanted to die. He thought that God did not care or love him any more. Disappointment should not discourage us like that.

I read about a rich man who suddenly lost almost all his money. He became so discouraged that he killed himself. Many people can laugh and smile only so long as they are healthy, and when they get an ache or a pain they want to give up. Sometimes boys and girls find that they have difficulty with their lessons in school. And there are those who hang their heads, become discouraged, and want to give up.

When things do not go right, let us keep on smiling. When you have no money look for ways to earn some. When you are sick keep a cheerful disposition. When the lessons are hard say to yourself, " I can and I will." Remember, " where there is a will there is a way." Jesus said, " Let your light shine." This light cannot shine when we are discouraged; it cannot shine through a cloudy face.

Some people are happy only when everything goes smoothly and they have no trouble. (Light the candle without the potassium in the wick.) It is easy for this candle to shine. There are the tallow, a good wick, a good match, and no wind to blow it out. That is the way it is with many people; they are bright and cheerful as long as everything goes right.

But there are some people who remain sweet and happy even if they are greatly disappointed. I visited a friend in a hospital who had tuberculosis of the bones. She had many painful operations. I called on her to cheer her in her trouble. She was in great pain, but she needed no cheering. She was the happiest person I had met in a long time. Nothing could dampen her spirit. (Transfer a drop of water to the candle with the potassium in the wick.) She was like this candle. Even water cannot keep this candle from shining. There are many good people in the world whom hardship and trouble cannot keep from smiling. One would think that water would never make this candle light. Many people are like this candle. They shine and they smile, nothing dampens their spirits.

No man faced more hardships than Abraham Lincoln. He had little education, and he lost his mother when he was a young lad. He failed in business and failed in politics many times. All this did not discourage him. It only made him all the more anxious to succeed. He finally became president of the United States. Water did not keep this one candle from shining. In fact, the water made it burn. Hardships did not make Lincoln give up. Instead of letting hardships and handicaps get him down, they made him the good man that he was.

39

DOING THE IMPOSSIBLE

Materials:

A hard-boiled egg with shell removed.
A quart milk bottle.
A small piece of paper.
A match.

Demonstration:

The mouth of the milk bottle is considerably smaller than the egg. The object is to make the egg go through the mouth of the milk bottle. When the egg is placed on the mouth of the bottle it would seem to be impossible. However, the seemingly impossible is possible. Set the bottle on the table. Light a small piece of paper and put it inside the bottle and place the egg on the mouth of the bottle, with the pointed end downward. A vacuum is created by the flaming paper and the egg is drawn into the bottle.

Story:

Can this egg go through the mouth of this bottle? It seems impossible, but it can be done. We do not want to force the egg through, because then we should break it. There are many things that seem impossible, but they are not.

Before we make the egg go through the mouth of this bottle, I want to tell you a story. In 1831 there was born in Ireland a baby who was called Arthur Kavanagh. This baby did not have arms and legs like the rest of us. He merely had little stumps for legs and arms, so that he really had no legs and arms at all. When Arthur Kavanagh was a boy he did not want to be pitied. He tried to do everything that any normal boy could do. When he was a young man he was one of the best riders. He traveled thousands of miles on horseback in Egypt, Palestine, Russia, Persia, and India. He had to be strapped into the saddle because he had no legs with which to hold on to the horse. He rode at a fast pace and would jump the highest fences with the best riders. Because he had no legs he went on horseback wherever he wanted to go. In the house he would go from room to room by a series of jumps and springs.

He was an expert hunter and went deep into the wilderness of India to hunt tigers and other wild animals. His ability to shoot straight surprised every one. Strapped in his saddle, he would rest his gun on the stump of his left leg and, with a hook which was fastened to the stump of the right arm, he would pull the trigger. He could shoot birds on the wing while his horse trotted at a good pace.

He was very intelligent and spoke several languages. Although he had no arms and, therefore, no fingers, he painted pictures and wrote many letters. Many people came to him for advice. The people thought so much of him that they sent him to the British Parliament.

25071

Because of his physical handicaps he might easily have become sour, but he was always cheerful. He loved all people and did much good. He often spoke of how good God had been to him. When he was a baby and without arms and legs, those who saw him must have said, " He cannot live, and if he does he will never amount to anything; it is impossible." But Arthur Kavanagh fooled them all. What seemed impossible he made possible. He depended on God to help him. Jesus once said, " With men this is impossible, but with God all things are possible."

Now, here I have two very simple things, a hard-boiled egg and a milk bottle. The egg is too big to go into the bottle. If we force the egg it will break. How shall we do it? There are some who would say it is impossible. But it can be done. I will get that egg in there with something that you cannot see. (Perform trick.) What seemed impossible has been done. What pulled the egg inside? The paper on fire? No. The fire burned all the air in the bottle. That made a vacuum. A vacuum is very strong, even if you cannot see it. What seemed to be impossible has been done.

God is the strongest person in the whole world. There is nothing impossible with Him. You cannot see God; neither could you see the vacuum in the bottle. Jesus did some wonderful things. He made the blind to see, the deaf to hear, and the lame to walk. Jesus did so many things that we would think were impossible. When the people asked Him how He could do all this, He answered, " With men this is impossible, but with God all things are possible." Let us ask God to help us with some of the things we think are impossible. Remember, He is the strongest one in the whole world. He helped Arthur Kavanagh with what seemed impossible. He helped Jesus. God can help us to do what seems impossible.

40

GOD OR MONEY

Materials:

A piece of paper two inches by three inches.
A pencil.
A handkerchief for a blindfold.

Demonstration:

Divide the piece of paper into three slips, each one inch by two inches, by tearing. Two of these slips will have three straight even sides and one rough side, and the other will have two irregular rough sides and two straight smooth sides. On the latter write the word " riches." On one of the others write " Christ," and on the other " no decision." Put these three slips into a hat. Have some one blindfold you, and then you proceed to draw out the slip of paper marked " riches." This can be done by the sense of touch, choosing the slip with the two rough and two smooth edges.

Story:

There lived in the land of Palestine about two thousand years ago a rich young man. This was at the time Jesus, our Saviour, lived in this same country. Jesus went about the country speaking to the people, healing the sick, and helping wherever He was needed. This rich young man watched Him with much interest; he admired His bravery and His actions so much that he wished to find out the secret of His way of living. So one night he secretly came to Jesus and asked Him, " Jesus, what can I do to be saved, what can I do to be more like you? " Quick as a flash came the answer from Jesus, " Sell all your property, give it to the poor, and come and follow me."

Do you know why Jesus wished him to sell all his property? Here is the reason. The young man loved his riches more than anything else in the world, more than his father and mother; yes, and worst of all, he loved his money more than he loved God. Here, indeed, was a decision for the rich young man to make. What was his answer to Jesus? (Perform trick.) See these three slips of paper; on one we will write " Christ," on the other, " riches," and on the third " no decision." Let us see what the young man decided. (Blindfolded, pick out the slip marked " riches.") Yes, the young man chose to keep his riches. He decided that he loved and needed them more than anything else, even more than he needed God.

Let us suppose that we were the rich young man and that we had to decide between love for God and love for money, what would we decide to do? Would we come to no decision? Would we choose, as the rich young man did, " riches "? Or would we say, " Yes, Jesus, we will follow you; we want to love God, as you do, more than anything else, even more than money and riches."

41

HOW TO PRAY

Materials:

Three newspaper rings.

Demonstration:

The rings are made from strips of paper about an inch in width. Use the double page of an opened newspaper. Paste together the two ends of the first strip, which will form the first ring. The second ring is formed by giving the strip a whole twist before pasting the ends, and the third ring by giving the strip a half twist before pasting.

When the first ring is cut into halves lengthwise (along its circumference), the result will be two separate and distinct rings. The second ring, when cut in the same manner, resolves itself into two interlinked rings; and the third ring when cut becomes one immense ring, twice the size of the former one. The twists in the second and third rings can be concealed by keeping the twists in the palm of the left hand.

Story:

These rings which I hold in my hands are very queer. They are similar to the prayer rings used by ancient priests. I have cut them from newspaper in order to have them as large as possible. Through a priest these prayer rings were consulted by the common people when they wished to know how God would answer their prayers.

Now, do you think that any common, ordinary person knew how to use and consult these prayer rings? The best thing we can do is to find out. (Ask some one to come up to try.) Now, George, if you cut this in two (hand him ring No. 1), how many rings will you have? Try it. (Give him scissors and show him how to cut it.) Of course, there are two rings, so I can see that you do not understand the prophecy of the priest. Shall I try?

(Cut ring No. 2.) Well, well, we have two rings locked together. That means that the prayer will receive the answer " yes." Shall I show you how the prayer ring will look if the answer is " no " ? Watch. (Cut ring No. 3.) If one large ring like this results, your prayer will be answered with " no."

Do we use or need prayer rings today? Of course not. And this is the reason. Over nineteen hundred years ago Jesus came to live in this world. He walked and talked and was here with us. He taught us many things while here. He taught us how to pray.

Did Jesus say, " Go to the priest and ask him to cut the prayer ring to see what the answer to your prayer will be " ? Oh, no! Jesus said, " When you pray say: Our Father, who art in heaven, etc." He told us to speak to and ask God directly when we pray.

Now, shall we bow our heads and pray the prayer which Jesus taught us?

42

HOW TO BE STRONG

Materials:

A candle.
A match.
A funnel.

Demonstration:

Demonstrate that if you blow through the small end of the funnel it is impossible to blow out the flame of the candle. Ask some one in the audience to extinguish the flame in this way. He will find it an impossible task. Then show how easy it is to extinguish the flame by blowing through the wide end of the funnel. Hold the funnel about two feet from the flame, with the small end pointed toward it.

Story:

(Perform trick.) Do you know why you cannot extinguish the flame when you blow through the small end of the funnel? The reason is that the current of air that you blow into it follows the sides of the cone-shaped part of the funnel. In other words, the current of air is scattered. When you blow through the wide end of the funnel the current of air at first is scattered, but as it travels on, it is all crowded through the small end of the funnel. When anything like that air is all brought together into one place it is called concentration.

You know what happens when you light a firecracker. There is a loud explosion. This is caused by the powder inside. If you took the powder out and scattered it on a board and then held a match to it, all it could do would be to sizzle a little and then go out. But when the powder is all brought together into one place and rolled up tightly in some strong paper then we have a firecracker, and a match held to it will cause it to explode. When the powder is brought together into one place that is concentration. It is the concentration which gives the powder its strength. It is so strong that we get badly hurt if we are too near at the time of the explosion. Scattered powder has no strength. Scattered air has no strength; it cannot even blow out the flame of a candle. But when we concentrate it and force it through the small end of the funnel it will easily extinguish the flame.

If we want to be strong we must concentrate. For example, when you are in school you cannot get your lessons if you are thinking first about this and then about that, when your mind should be upon your lesson. When you do this your thinking is scattered and it is impossible to get your lessons with scattered thinking. There is no strength in scattered thinking, no more than there is strength in scattered air or scattered powder. But when you concentrate your mind on the lesson before you and keep everything else out, then your mind is strong and you are able to do the lesson.

The person who works at this job today and does a different job tomorrow can never expect to be very good at any one of them. He has scattered himself over too many jobs. But if he would concentrate on one job he would become very good in that work; perhaps he would become an expert in it so that others would come to him to ask how it is done.

There are some people who like to go to one church this Sunday and to another on the next. They have scattered their church attendance over too much territory, and the result is that if they are absent from one church nobody misses them. They cannot work in so many churches, and the result is that they do not work in any church. But if we go to one church and work in that church, then we can really do some good. We will have many friends in that church, and if we should have to be absent we would be missed. We should concentrate on one church and be loyal to it. We are strong only when we concentrate.

In the Ten Commandments God says to us, " Thou shalt have no other gods before me." There is only one God and we must be faithful and loyal to Him. We know what this God is like because we see Him in Jesus

Christ. God wants us to love Him more than anything else in this whole world. If we love anything else more than God, then we have made that our god. We are to have only one God, the God of Jesus Christ. We must not scatter our love on all kinds of gods, we must concentrate our love on the one true God. Our religion will give us strength when it is centered in or concentrated on the one God.

We can be strong if we concentrate with our minds, if we concentrate on one job, if we concentrate on one church, and if we concentrate on one God.

43

CHOOSING WISDOM

Materials:

Six cards, two by three inches in size. These may be cut from index filing cards.

Demonstration:

Number each card in the upper left corner, and put the same number on the lower right corner. On the reverse side of the cards write near the top these words: *Friends, Health, Wisdom, Pleasure, Wealth, Long Life.* And on the bottom of this reserve side write on each card the word *Wisdom.* The numbers on the bottom of the cards and the word *Wisdom* on the reverse side should be written so that they will not be upside down when the cards are turned end for end. Hold the cards with the numbers toward the audience and the side with the words toward yourself and with that end to the bottom on which the word *Wisdom* is written. Hold the cards in one hand, spreading them as wide as possible in a fanlike shape, and hold your thumb over the word *Wisdom* at the bottom to hide them. Show your helper the reverse side of the cards, being careful to hide the words at the bottom, and ask him to read the words at the top. Then shuffle the cards. Now spread them wide in a fanlike shape again and ask him to choose a card and to remember the number on the card he has chosen. As the selection is indicated, let your thumb slip down along to the lower corner of the selected card and, with your thumb hidden behind the cards, turn over a small corner. Shuffle the cards again. You can readily identify your helper's choice by the turned-over corner. As you show him the reverse side turn the card so that the word *Wisdom* is at the top and hide the word at the bottom with your thumb.

Story:

We go to school, and read books and magazines so that we may learn much. What can be better than to know many, many things? No one can ever know too much. But you may know much and not be wise. I will try to explain what I mean. A man may have studied hard in school, have read much, and may know most of the answers to the questions you ask him. But one day he drives in the country with his automobile, and it is wet and slippery. There are signs along the road warning him that the road is slippery when wet. But he drives fast and pays no attention to the signs. Suddenly he has an accident, killing his wife and breaking a bone in his little daughter's arm. That man knew much, but he was not wise. He did not have wisdom.

All the things you read in books cannot give you wisdom. But every one can have wisdom if he wants it.

For example, some one says something which hurts you. Now, you may be a bright and quick boy or girl, and you could say something in a flash that would hurt him much more than he hurt you. And if you did that you would show that you are quick and bright, but it would also show that you are not wise. You may show intelligence by doing that, but you do not show wisdom.

I read of a vicious dog attacking a small girl. A young boy saw this. What was he to do? If he should hit the dog, the dog would attack him. So he took off his coat and wrapped it around his fist and arm and held the dog off with his protected arm until help came. That is wisdom. He was a wise boy.

(Perform trick. Show your helper the reverse side of card he has selected, holding your thumb over bottom word. Ask him to read what is at the top, which will be the word *Wisdom*. Then address yourself to your helper.) Out of these six cards you have chosen a card with the word *Wisdom* on it. We should do well if we all would choose wisdom. Once there was a great king whose name was Solomon. He did not ask God for riches or a long life. He asked God to give him wisdom. And God made him a very wise man.

One day two mothers came to him with two babies. One baby was dead and the other was alive. Both mothers claimed the living child. The wise King Solomon listened to both mothers. Then he said, " Bring me a sword." When the sword was brought in he said, " Take the sword and cut the living child in two, and give half of it to each mother." Then one mother said, " Do not kill my child. Let the other woman have it, but let the child live." But the other mother said, " Cut the child in two, and divide it between us." Then the wise king knew that the woman who did not want the baby killed was the true mother, and he gave her the child. He was a very wise man.

Solomon prayed God to give him wisdom. So we, too, may have wisdom if we ask God for it.

44

MAKING YOUR LIFE COUNT

Materials:

An empty pay envelope of the type which has the flap at the end.

A quarter.

Two pennies.

Demonstration:

Before the demonstration place the two pennies in the envelope. Just above the pennies, which are resting in the bottom, cut a slit across the envelope on the opposite side to the flap. The palm of the hand holding the envelope should be toward you, with the flap pointing upward. A slight squeeze on the envelope sides will open the slit. Drop the quarter into the envelope, which will slide through the slit and into your hand. Seal the envelope and hold it up in the other hand. This gives you an opportunity to dispose of the quarter. Then tearing the envelope into several pieces, the two pennies are produced, and the quarter has mysteriously disappeared.

Story:

When a wise person has saved some money he does

not spend it on all sorts of foolish things. There are some people who do that, and in the end they have nothing to show for it.

Jesus told of a young man who had received a large sum of money from his father. What do you suppose he did with it? He went into a far country and spent it foolishly and in a bad way until it was all gone. He had nothing to show for it. And then he was in great trouble, but fortunately his father welcomed him home again. But a wise person will not waste his money; he will put his money where it can do the most good.

God has given each one of us a life. What shall we do with it? If it is necessary to put our money where it can do the most good, how much more important it is to put our lives where they can do the most good. After all, your life has more value than anything else in the world. Jesus told us that again and again.

We all know how easy it is to waste money on cheap things and then in the end have nothing. It is also very easy to do that with our lives. Here is a good quarter of a dollar. Watch carefully to see what happens to it. (Perform demonstration.) The quarter is gone and all I have left is two pennies. That is the way money can easily be frittered away. But what is many, many times worse than that is when our lives are frittered away.

How can you put your life where it can do the most good? Let me tell you how George Washington Carver, a Negro boy, did it. He was born of parents who were slaves. He never knew his father, and his mother was taken away when he was a baby. The first ten years of his life he never attended school. Then he had to work to get enough money to stay in school. One week he lived on ten cents; he bought five cents' worth of corn meal and five cents' worth of suet and that is all the food he had for an entire week. But he worked hard, and finally became a teacher in Tuskegee Institute in Alabama. The Negroes in Alabama were very poor. Whole families lived in small one-room cabins. Every one in the families, including the small children, worked hard in the cotton fields.

So Mr. Carver decided to do something for these poor Negroes. How do you think he did it? He had become a great scientist, and from sweet potatoes he made flour, paste, breakfast foods, coffee, candy, dyes, starch, vinegar, ink, shoe blacking, molasses, and wood filler. He also discovered that many products could be made from peanuts, which grow abundantly in Alabama. With these discoveries Mr. Carver sent many Negroes to new jobs, so that they could live better and be more comfortable. One result is that new schools, churches, and libraries have been built.

Mr. Carver put his life where it could do the most good. He never boasted about all the good he had done. He always said that God was doing this through him. He taught a Bible class for many years.

We, too, must put our lives where they can do the most good. Do not waste your life on things that are not important. Make your life count. God wants you to do something for Him in this world. There is so much to do. What do you want to be and what do you want to do? You should be thinking about that now.

Find out what you can do best and where you can do the most good. Make up your mind as soon as possible and then start getting ready for the job you want to do. Get the best education you can, work

hard, and keep your goal in mind and your life will
not be frittered away.

45

GOD SAVES THE PIECES

Materials:

An octagonal pencil.
A dollar bill.

Demonstration:

Have some one hold the pencil firmly between both
hands, placing each hand near the ends of the pencil
and extending the arm slightly forward. Then fold
your dollar bill lengthwise and grasp it with the right
hand close to the end, and announce that you will
break the pencil with the dollar bill. Then raise the
right hand, and as you bring it downward extend the
index finger so that the finger hits the pencil and breaks
it. This must be done quickly so that the audience
does not see the extended forefinger, and as soon as
the pencil is broken the finger should be returned
immediately to its original position.

Story:

For this story I will need a helper, a strong boy,
I think. John, will you come up here to help me? Hold
this pencil, please. (Show him how to hold it; produce
dollar bill.) Now, what do you suppose I am going
to do with this dollar bill? You will never guess, so
watch. (Perform trick.)

One day I saw a boy break a nice new pencil. Thinking the pieces were of no value, he threw them away. But two poor children walking along picked up the pieces and made use of them. They had been rejected, thrown away, but some one made use of them.

For eight years I watched a ragpicker, a garbage scavenger, go from garbage can to basket of refuse and glean out certain things. Articles which to every one seemed broken and useless he would salvage. Last spring the newspaper in the city in which he lived carried this headline: " The Loveliest Wedding of the Season." Who do you suppose the bride was? She was the daughter of the ragpicker who had collected the articles others had discarded and had not only made a living but had become a respectable citizen.

Many, many years ago in the country of Italy there lived a sculptor, Donatello by name, who was chiseling away on an immense piece of marble. Suddenly he discovered a flaw, a crack. " That marble is of no use any more," he said. " I will throw it away." So it was thrown into his back yard. Some time later the great artist and sculptor Michael Angelo walked by this yard and saw this discarded piece of marble lying there. He saw its possibilities and had it taken to his studio. From this discarded, cracked stone Michael Angelo carved one of his greatest masterpieces, the statue of David. Was it useless, this stone, because it was cracked and broken?

Sometimes we feel as if our lives are broken, just as the pencil was, and that we are useless. Edison, for instance, became deaf, but God made use of him. Franklin D. Roosevelt was crippled by infantile paralysis, but he became president of our country. The apostle Paul contended with ill health (a thorn in the flesh), but God made of him a mighty man in the kingdom.

So we have no reason to be discouraged, for God says, " I can make use of the pieces."

46

GOALS IN LIFE

Materials:

An ounce of saltpeter.
A tumbler filled with warm water.
A fine brush.
A sheet of typewriter paper (unglazed).
A small rod with facilities to heat one end.

Demonstration:

The sheet of paper should be prepared beforehand. On the right-hand side of the sheet, near the top, write the words *Great Riches*. Two inches below write the words *Strong Body*. Then the words *Christian Life;* next *Good Mind* and, finally, *Great Fame*. On the left-hand side of the sheet, directly opposite the words *Christian Life,* write the name *John*. Dip the fine brush into the saltpeter solution and draw a circle directly around the words *Christian Life*. Then draw a line from this circle directly toward the name *John*. Then from the name *John* draw diverging lines toward each of the other words, stopping within an inch of them. The saltpeter solution on the paper will soon dry and become invisible. Touch with a hot iron the point near the name *John*, from which the lines diverge. The outline you draw will start to fizz. On the seemingly blank paper will unfold the entire sketch. It is very important that you leave no gaps when you apply the saltpeter solution.

Story:

The words on the right-hand side of the paper are certain goals in life. (Show paper.) You all know what a goal is. When you enter a race you know that at the other end is the goal, and that the one who gets there first wins the race. But there are many other kinds of goals. A goal is something that you try to reach. For example, every boy has as his goal to be a man some day. When he has become a full-grown man he has reached that goal. But every boy and girl should have a higher goal than just to grow up.

On the left-hand side of this sheet I have written the name *John*. On the other side are five goals which John has before him.

John could strive for the first goal, great riches. Some people want to get very rich. This is their main goal. They want money to buy everything and anything they want. Some will be dishonest and will deceive in order to get more money. There are others who get their money honestly, but they are so absorbed in earning money that they have no time for friends, laughter, and enjoyment. They have no time to go to church or to think of God. Very often, when such people get old, they are lonely and friendless. All their lives they have worked for money, and when they die they cannot take it into the next world. No, money should not be our goal in life. Most of us will not be very rich in money.

John could have as his goal in life a strong body. It is a great blessing to have a strong, healthy body. Jesus Himself made people strong and well. But a man is more than his body. John may strive to have a strong body, but he will never be as strong as some of the animals, such as the horse or the elephant. Some people live for their bodies. Eating is one of their main interests. We all want strong bodies, but that is not our main goal. All people do not have strong bodies.

We will omit the third goal now, and come back to it later. The fourth goal before John is a good mind. We go to school to study and to improve our minds. We need people who can think clearly. We all need better minds. We should do everything we can to have better minds. But no matter how much we know, we still know very little. Most of us cannot have great minds.

The fifth goal before John is great fame. It is splendid to be world famous like George Washington, Abraham Lincoln, and Charles Lindbergh. But most of us will not reach the goal of great fame.

But all of us can reach the third goal, the Christian Life. This goal, too, is before John. (Perform trick.) According to this sketch, John never reached the goal of great riches. He did not have the strongest body or the greatest mind. He did not become famous. But he did reach the most important goal, the Christian Life. We, too, may not reach the other goals but we can all be Christians. When we follow Jesus we are Christians. This we can all do, as John did. This should be the main goal in life. Jesus' invitation is, " Come and follow me." By this Jesus means that He wants us to live as He lived. If we do this we are truly Christian.

47

GOD CLEANSES THE SPOTS

Materials:

Magic thumb or a thimble large enough to fit thumb. It must be painted flesh color.

Piece of spotted or dotted china silk about four inches square.

Piece of black china silk about four inches square.

Demonstration:

Have magic thumb on your right thumb. Close hand into a fist and place the handkerchief over it. Slip right thumb, on which is the magic thumb, into closed left hand, pushing handkerchief with your right thumb partly into left fist. Allow the magic thumb to remain in closed left hand. Remove right thumb. Then show the piece of spotted material, which represents the spotted disease of leprosy. With your right thumb push it into the magic thumb in your left fist, at the same time explaining how Jesus made the leprosy disappear.

Now show the piece of black silk. This black silk represents the shadow of sin which is over us all. As Jesus made the leprosy disappear, so also can God, through Jesus, make our sins to disappear if we ask for forgiveness. Then push the black silk into the magic thumb, and at the same time push the magic thumb on the right thumb, so that when the right thumb is withdrawn, the magic thumb will be withdrawn also. Seize the handkerchief with your right hand, keeping right thumb concealed behind one corner. Shake the handkerchief, and the spotted and black pieces of silk will have mysteriously disappeared. The magic thumb may be slipped into your pocket at the first opportunity.

Story:

Once, as Jesus was going into a village, He saw ten men standing afar off. They were afflicted with the terrible disease of leprosy. Have you boys and girls ever had measles? If so, you were quarantined for several weeks, were you not? These poor lepers were quarantined for life, they were not allowed to come near people who did not have leprosy. So they called to Jesus from a distance, " Jesus, Master, have mercy on us, help us! "

No wonder they wanted Jesus to help them. Leprosy was a dreadful disease. There was no cure for it, people broke out with it on any part of their body. They were not allowed to live with their families but had to leave their homes and live with other lepers.

And when Jesus saw these ten lepers, He said, " Go, show yourselves to the priests." So the ten men traveled on. All at once they noticed that they were well and strong. They were no longer lepers. Their skin was like that of a healthy child. How happy they must have been. They were no longer lepers, they could go back to their homes, to their parents, to their brothers and sisters. Jesus had made them well.

(Perform trick.) Do you see this spotted piece of silk? Let us say that it represents leprosy. You know, when you had measles you had little spots on your bodies; so men that had leprosy had spots all over their bodies. Jesus made the lepers well, did He not? He caused the spots to disappear. Now watch. (Push spotted silk into magic thumb as explained.) See, the leprosy has disappeared.

Here we have a piece of black silk. Any sin or wrong
which we do is like this black silk, which represents
the shadow of sin which is over us all. Can we get
rid of this shadow? Shall I tell you how? We must
let Jesus come into our lives and ask Him to help us in
our fight against sin. If we do this the shadow of sin
will disappear as this black silk disappears. (Now
push the black silk into the magic thumb and finish the
trick as explained in the demonstration.) I'd like to
have you remember this little poem:

> " Do your best, your very best,
> And do it every day;
> Little boys and little girls,
> That's the wisest way." *

48

THE GREAT MIND READER

Materials:

A sheet of paper and a pencil.

Demonstration:

Ask your helper to think of some number and have
him write it on the sheet of paper large enough so that
when he holds it toward the audience they can see it.
The object is for you to ascertain the number your
helper has in mind. Bid him double that number and
then multiply this product by five. Ask him what the
final answer is. If you cut off the last figure from
this, the number left will be the original number your
helper had in mind. If the number thought of be

* See footnote, page 92.

thirteen, which doubled makes twenty-six, that multiplied by five produces one hundred thirty. Then if you take away the last figure you have the number thought of.

Story:

There are people who are called mind readers. They are supposed to be able to tell you what you are thinking about. Do you think this can be done? Let us try it.

I will ask my helper to write a number on this sheet of paper. (Hand him the paper and pencil.) I want him to write it large enough so that when he holds it toward you, you can see the number. But he must not show me the number. I want to tell you the number my helper thought of without seeing it. (Instruct your helper to do as it is explained in the demonstration.) Well, it seems as if I can read his mind. Do you think that I really read his mind? No, I must be honest, I did not read his mind. I got the right number because he did what I asked him to do. If he had not given me this information, I could never have done it.

No one on earth can tell what you are thinking about. You think with your mind. God has given us minds so that we can think. You cannot say something good unless you first think good; you cannot say anything bad unless you first think bad. I cannot tell by looking at you whether you are thinking about something good or bad. Of course, if you should have an angry look on your face I know at once that you are thinking angry thoughts. But I cannot read your mind to see what makes you angry. And if you are happy and smiling I know that you have pleasant thoughts in your mind. But I cannot read your mind to see what makes you happy. I cannot know what makes you angry or what makes you happy unless you tell me.

There are some people who are called fortune tellers. They pretend that by looking at you they can tell you what will happen to you and what kind of a person you will be. Many people are foolish enough to go to them.

There is only one person who can tell what will happen to you and what kind of person you will become. That person is God. He is the greatest mind reader. He is the only one that can really read our minds. God can read our thoughts before we put them into words. He knows whether we are thinking evil or good thoughts.

The apostle John said of Jesus: "He knew what was in man." This means that Jesus can read our minds. One day Jesus came to a city called Sychar. There was a well there, and Jesus, being tired, sat down on the wall of the well. A woman came to draw water from the well, and Jesus began a conversation with her. This woman had done many things that were wrong; she was living a life of which she might well be ashamed. She was ashamed of herself and she thought that Jesus was like other people and would not know about her past. But Jesus could read her mind. He told her all about herself. She was a very surprised woman. She hurried back into the city and said to the people: "Come, see a man who knows everything that I have ever done."

Yes, God knows everything we have ever done. When we have done something that is not right we can, perhaps, keep it hidden from other people. But we are only fooling ourselves. We cannot keep it hidden from God. He is the Great Mind Reader.

49

"I THANK THEE, LORD"

(THANKSGIVING)

Materials:

Tincture of tannin.

Tincture of iron.

Oxalic acid.

Ammonia.

Hydrochloric acid. (These chemicals may be obtained in any drug store.)

Ten small tumblers half filled with water.

Demonstration:

For best results the performer should experiment beforehand. Add a small portion of tincture of tannin to the water in each glass. A few drops of tincture of iron will turn the liquid black. Stir well. Then add a bit of oxalic acid which has been dissolved in water. This will restore the original clearness of the water. When a little ammonia is added, the water will turn a deep red. Finally, put a little hydrochloric acid into one of the glasses, and the mixture in it will again become clear.

Story:

(The tincture of tannin should be in the water of the ten glasses before beginning the story.) One time, as Jesus was walking through a village, ten lepers stood at a distance and called to Him to cure them. These ten glasses represent the ten lepers. Leprosy is a loathsome skin disease. Those ten lepers had been as clean and as healthy as the water in these ten glasses. But now they had a bad disease. Their skin was full of ulcers and sores. They were sick and lonesome; no one would associate with them. (Add the tincture of iron.) Life for them was black, black as this water. Jesus took pity on the ten lepers and healed them all. (Add some of the oxalic acid.) And now they were as healthy and as clean as before. They were cleansed like this water. And all ten of them started to walk away, with not even a " Thank you " to Jesus. How ungrateful they were. (Add some ammonia.) The water has turned to crimson. This crimson color stands for the sin of unthankfulness on the part of these lepers. The prophet Isaiah talked about sin being " red like crimson." One of the worst sins is ingratitude to God; that sin is " red like crimson." But one of the lepers thought better of it, and so he turned back to thank God for what Jesus had done to him. (Add some hydrochloric acid to one glass only.) When this one leper thanked God, the sin of ingratitude was forgiven by Jesus, and he became clean and pure in his soul like this water. This one leper not only had his body healed, he also had his soul cleansed of the sin of ingratitude. But though the bodies of the other nine were healed, their souls were still " red like crimson " with the sin of ingratitude.

We should thank God every day. There is a story * about a good servant who worked for his master for many years. Just before the master died, he gave the servant a magic bag in which there were food, drink, clothing, and many other things which he needed. The master also gave him four magic words. These he

* " The Four Lost Words," from *Query Queer,* by Jay T. Stocking. Copyright, The Pilgrim Press. Used by permission.

whispered into his ear. So long as the servant remembered these magic words his bag would always remain full.

Then the servant went on a long journey, and wherever he went, he found the things he needed in the magic bag, because he remembered the four magic words. But after a while he did not think so much about the four magic words, and, finally, he forgot them completely. The bag was nearly empty and the magic words were gone.

He went on to a certain town where lived a wise man, and asked him what the four magic words might be. " The four magic words," said Mr. Wiseman, are: " I wish I had." Then the servant thanked him, and repeated the words:

> " I wish I had, I wish I had,
>   I wish I had as much
>   As all my friends and neighbors have
>   Of health and wealth and such."

But when he looked at his bag it was as empty as before.

Another wise man told him that the four magic words were " Give me some more." The servant thanked him and repeated these words:

> " Give me some more, give me some more,
>   Give me some more, much more.
>   O fill my bag of blessings up
>   As full as it was before."

But even these words did not fill his bag.

Then the servant flung his bag over his shoulder and started down the street. He met two children, who were cold and hungry. Although his bag was nearly empty he gave the children a little to eat and a little to wear. He was glad he had a little to share with these poor children. As he turned he saw that he was standing near a church. He knelt on the steps and prayed:

> " I thank thee, Lord, I thank thee, Lord;
> I thank thee, Lord, once more
> For all the blessings in my bag,
> O Lord, how great a store."

As he prayed, he suddenly remembered that these were the magic words: " I thank thee, Lord." He looked at his bag and it was full.

God will take care of all those who do not forget to thank Him. The four magic words are " I thank thee, Lord." That is what the one leper said.

50

A STRANGE MIXTURE

Materials:

Two tablespoons of Epsom salts mixed in one-fourth cup of water.

Two tablespoons potassium carbonate mixed in one-fourth cup of water. (The potassium carbonate may be secured in any drug store.)

Demonstration:

The two solutions should be well mixed in separate tumblers. Allow them to stand a while until they are perfectly clear. Pour the two solutions together and they will at once become a squashy solid. Do not stir after the two solutions are poured together.

Story:

There are some things that you cannot mix without danger. If you should mix fire and gasoline there would be a big explosion and you would be badly hurt and perhaps be killed. If you should put a mixture of gasoline and water into the tank of the automobile it would not start. If you eat very sweet candy and then eat a very sour pickle, you will have cramps and bad pains, because candy and pickles do not mix well.

It looks as if I had two good drinks in these glasses. I will mix them together. (Pour the two solutions together.) See what has happened! No, I cannot drink it at all; it has formed into a squashy solid. This will never satisfy my thirst. Those two liquids when mixed together just cannot make a good drink.

The lesson that we should learn from these two glasses of water is that we should not try to mix certain things. Remember what happens when you mix candy and pickles or gasoline and fire.

Jesus said that there are people who are like wolves in sheep's clothing. You know what a wolf is like. He is a wild, dangerous beast. But a sheep is a very harmless and fine animal. Imagine a wolf putting on the skin of a sheep in order to look like a sheep. A wolf inside a sheep's skin! What a fine-looking sheep he would be. If you mix a wolf and a sheep together you will still have a wolf.

Have you ever heard the fable of the wolf in sheep's clothing? Let me tell it to you. One day a wolf was very hungry. He thought and thought and thought, " How can I satisfy my hunger? " And finally he had

an idea. What do you suppose he did? A month or
so before he had killed a large sheep. So he took the
skin of that sheep and draped it over his body. Now,
he thought to himself, " I look like a sheep. I'll go over
into that field among that big flock of sheep, they won't
know me, for I am disguised and I'll be able to kill and
eat many of them." The shepherd noticed that many
of his sheep were disappearing, and one day he discovered the reason. So he fastened a rope around the
pretended sheep's neck, led him to a tree, and there
hanged him. You see, he tried to be both a wolf and a
sheep, which was not possible.

Now, Jesus said that some people want to be a wolf
at heart and look like a sheep from the outside. The
wolf has a bad nature, the sheep a good nature. If we
try to mix the bad and the good we get into trouble.
If we are bad at heart like a wolf, and try to look like
a sheep from the outside, we are like a wolf in sheep's
clothing. You cannot mix wolf and sheep.

The water which I had in the two glasses did not
mix well. See what happened to it? That is what
happens when we try to mix good and bad. The boy
or girl who says I will be good in church, sing the
hymns, and worship God, but the rest of the week,
when I am with others where my friends cannot see me,
I will do anything I please—such a boy or girl is trying
to mix good and bad. In the end such a person will
get into trouble. He is like a wolf who tries to look
like a sheep.

Bad people and good people cannot live in the same
house. They simply do not mix well. Either the bad
people or the good people will have to move out. Good
and bad cannot live in your heart. Do not try to keep
both in your heart. They will not mix. Keep out the

bad and let only the good come in and you will be happy. Do not try to mix the bad with the good.

51

TWO-FACED

Materials:

Two band rings.
One pencil.
Two men's handkerchiefs.

Demonstration:

A borrowed ring is wrapped in a handkerchief and given to the helper to hold. The performer asks the helper, " Do you feel the ring? " Of course, the helper feels the ring in the prepared handkerchief. The performer then gives a pencil to the helper. A handkerchief is thrown over the pencil. The performer then grasps a corner of each handkerchief, the one enfolding the ring and the one covering the pencil, and gives each a sharp pull. The ring has vanished from the handkerchief and has mysteriously gotten onto the pencil.

The performer must prepare for this trick by sewing a plain ring in one corner of a handkerchief and covering it with a piece of the same material. When he wraps up the borrowed ring, he really keeps it in his hand and wraps up the sewed-in ring instead. He then takes the pencil and while walking over to the helper, slips the borrowed ring on the center, holding the ring between his thumb and his first two fingers, the thumb being uppermost. In this position the ring will be completely hidden from sight and the performer's grip on the pencil will look perfectly natural. As the performer hands the pencil to the helper, he must warn him to hold it level. As soon as the handkerchief is thrown over the pencil, the performer removes his hand, but not before, and the trick is brought to a rapid conclusion lest the person holding the pencil tilt it and discover the hidden ring.

Story:

One day I saw a queer thing. You'll never be able to guess what it was. So I'll tell you. It was a dog with two heads. Where his tail was supposed to be, he had an artificial head. He walked across the stage in a theater. I watched him for some time but could not determine which was the real head and which the artificial.

All of you have heard of Robert Louis Stevenson who wrote the poem " How do you like to go up in a swing? " and the boys all like to read his adventure story, *Treasure Island.* Stevenson wrote another story, called *Dr. Jekyll and Mr. Hyde.* Dr. Jekyll mixed up a potion made up of drugs, drank it, and became Mr. Hyde. While he was his real self, Dr. Jekyll, he was a good, kind and helpful man, but as soon as he drank the potion he became Mr. Hyde, who was a wicked man. He turned from the right to the left.

(Perform trick.) Is this not a strange ring? It went from the handkerchief in my helper's right hand to the pencil in his left hand. What a queer ring! We don't know what to think of it. Neither do we know what to think of Dr. Jekyll. Today he is good Dr. Jekyll, but tomorrow wicked Mr. Hyde.

Judas, the disciple of Jesus, was also two-faced.

While he was with Jesus he was His friend, but when he was with others he was Jesus' enemy. He went from the right to the left, just as the ring did. Some people are nice to us, but talk about us behind our backs. They are just like this ring. Boys and girls promise to help in church, in Sunday school or in the choir but they find excuses. They are like Dr. Jekyll, they turn from the right to the left. They also closely resemble this ring, do they not?

52

APPEARANCES ARE DECEIVING

Materials:

A nickel.

A penny.

A small match box with a sliding drawer.

Demonstration:

Pull out the sliding drawer of the match box almost all the way. Give it to the audience for examination. When it is returned to you, grasp the match box in your right hand, with the extended drawer down. The back of your right hand should be toward the audience, and hold the match box so that its bottom side is toward you. In the palm of the right hand you have concealed a penny, and the open drawer is brought directly over it. The penny can easily be dropped into the drawer by a twist of the hand. Borrow a nickel from some one, and with your left hand drop it into the open end of the match box cover. At the same time, with the little finger of the left hand push the drawer into the closed position, and the nickel that you drop into the cover will be ejected secretly into the palm of your left hand. Pass the match box to some one in the audience. When he opens the drawer he will be greatly surprised to find a penny instead of a nickel.

Story:

(Perform the trick and then tell the story.) Do you really believe that the nickel turned into a penny? Of course you don't. You know that by some trick I took out the nickel you saw me drop into the box and put a penny in its place. I cannot change a nickel into a penny. It may look as if I did, but really I did not.

You must not let looks fool you. Appearances are deceiving. I will try to explain what I mean by that. Out in the woods and open fields there are all kinds of wild berries in the summer. The color of these berries is beautiful and there are many shades. Most of the berries are good to eat, and when boys and girls see them they want to pick them. But there are some of those lovely colored berries that are not good to eat; they are poison, and if you eat them you will become very ill. These poisonous berries look good but they are not good. Do not let looks fool you. It looked as if I changed a nickel into a penny. It only looked that way; I fooled you.

A wolf looks different from a sheep. There is an old fable which tells us that one day a wolf put on the skin of a sheep in order to look like a sheep. In this way the wolf got in among the sheep and killed some of them. The shepherd began to miss these sheep, and at last discovered that among his flock was a wolf in a sheep's skin. So he put a rope around his neck and hanged him. The wolf at first fooled the shepherd, but not for long.

We should not try to fool others by our looks. There are people who want to fool us by their looks. A good-looking suit cannot make a bad boy a good boy any more than a sheep's skin can make a wolf a sheep. A nice bright dress cannot make a bad girl a good girl. The suit and the dress are not important. It is the boy inside the suit or the girl inside the dress that counts. The Bible tells us that God does not look at the outward appearance, but that He looks into your heart. If the heart is all right then everything else is all right. If the heart is good, then you do not have to pretend to be what you are not.

I may be able to fool you into thinking that I have turned a nickel into a penny; the poison berry may look beautiful; the wolf in a sheep's skin may look like a sheep, but do not be fooled or tricked by looks. Beautiful berries can be poisonous and a wolf in a sheep's skin is not to be trusted. We may be able to fool others but we cannot fool God, because He looks right through us into our hearts.

53

HEARTS FILLED WITH LOVE
(CHRISTMAS)

Materials:

Two small match boxes.

Demonstration:

All the matches are removed from both boxes. To

prepare for this demonstration, the performer removes the label from one match box and pastes it on the bottom of the other. The top and the bottom of the prepared box will then be identical. Wedge a layer of matches between the bottom of the drawer and the bottom of the box. To do this break down the bottom of the drawer just enough so that the matches will be flush with the sides of the drawer. This one layer of matches will give the appearance of a full box of matches when the drawer is partly opened. By turning the box over and opening the drawer partly, it will amaze the spectators to find it empty. If you occasionally turn the box in your hand as you talk and before you open the drawer to show when it is empty and when it is full, it will prevent the audience from detecting that the box has been especially prepared. You should have a secret mark on the box to know which side is which.

Story:

Christmas is a gloriously happy time. It is a time of greetings and giving. At the first Christmas it was God who gave us Jesus. God likes to give. He gave us many, many wonderful things long before He gave us Jesus. God gave us everything that is in this world. Everything in this whole universe was created by God. God made the sun, stars, trees, flowers, grass, and all things beautiful. He did not buy these ready made. He made them. No one but God could have made them. And then He gave them all to us. God is always giving. He has a heart full of love, and a heart filled with love likes to give. The best gift that God gave us is Jesus. And the day He was born we call Christmas. That is why Christmas is such a happy day.

But some people are not happy, even at Christmas. It is because their hearts are empty—empty of love. Look at this match box. (Open drawer to show empty side.) It is empty and that is the way many people's hearts are. Joy comes from a heart full of love. If the heart is full of love there will be joy. (Open drawer again to show full side.) The box now seems to be full of matches. Even so, a person who a while ago was unhappy because there was no love in his heart can suddenly overflow with joy if he will let God fill his heart with love. God spreads happiness not only on Christmas but on every day, because He loves all of us. " For God so loved the world that he gave his only begotten Son."

Whose hearts are empty of love at Christmas and whose hearts are not empty? Let us look at a few people. Here are a husband and wife who on Christmas day are standing in front of a beautiful new house that they have just built. " I don't like the paint," says the wife, " it is terrible. And I don't like the way the kitchen is arranged." The husband becomes angry and says, " I don't care whether you like it or not; it is bought and paid for, you can take it or leave it." With that he walks away. (Show empty side of match box.) Their hearts are empty of love just as this match box is empty. The trouble with these two people is that they have selfishly spent everything they had on their house for themselves. Even on Christmas day they had nothing to give to others. Their hearts are empty.

Not far away there are another husband and wife, who have been saving up money for a new automobile. They looked at some of the newest shiny models shortly before Christmas. " What do you think of this one? " said the husband. " I like this one the best, especially the color." The wife does not seem to be very enthusiastic about any of the automobiles. " What is the matter? " asks the husband. " Don't you want a new automobile? " " Well," says the wife, " I don't think I want one just now. Here it is almost Christmas. If we buy a new automobile we will have no money left to buy gifts for others, especially some of the poor people who need clothes, food, and coal to keep them warm. We can make our old automobile do for a while. I think I will be happier with the old automobile during the Christmas holidays than with a new one." " Perhaps you are right," says the husband. " Let us see what kind of gifts we can find to make others happy." (Show full side of match box.) These two people were truly happy because their hearts were full of love, even as this match box is full of matches.

In another house is a boy who is very excited on the day before Christmas. He says to his playmate, who has never received much for Christmas, " In that room are a bicycle, skates, an electric train, and many other things, all for me. Tomorrow I will let you see them, but don't you touch them." (Show empty side of match box.) This boy's heart is empty of all love. He is thinking only of himself.

But in the next house lives a boy who is on his way to the store on the day before Christmas. He is whistling as he hurries along. He comes out of the store with two packages. One contains a nice new necktie for his father, and the other a scarf for his mother. He has earned the money to buy these by selling newspapers and shoveling walks. It has taken him a long time to save so much money. As he hides them in the closet he says, " Oh, boy, won't they be

surprised tomorrow? "   (Show full side of match box.)
This boy is happy because his heart is full of love.

Christmas will be a very happy occasion if we do
something for others. But remember this—we cannot
do good from an empty heart. God always gives and
always does good because His heart is full of love for us.

54

THE LIGHT OF THE WORLD

Materials:

A candle.
A glass jar (large enough to cover candle).

Demonstration:

Place the jar over the lighted candle, and the lack of
oxygen will soon extinguish the flame.

Story:

Do you boys and girls know who was called the Light
of the World?   Yes, you are right, it was Jesus. Would
you all like to be " lights in the world " ? If you would
like to be a " light " you must try to be like Jesus.

Now, in what way or ways can we be like Jesus?
Let us think of some of the things which Jesus did. He
tried to make others happy, did He not? One day He
called at the home of a man named Jairus, whose little
daughter Tabitha was very ill. When He arrived there,
Tabitha had died and every one was weeping and was
very sad. But Jesus said, " Wake up, Tabitha," and
Tabitha awoke. Oh, how happy her parents were!

Can you, like Jesus, make others happy? I once knew a little boy, four years of age, who was called "Sunshine" by all the grown-ups and children. Do you know why? He was always smiling. Can you smile? Let me see. Oh, yes, you all know how, don't you? Will you practice that every day? I am sure every one who comes near you will be happy, and then you will be a "light."

We also can be "lights" if we try to help children who are less fortunate than we. Suppose we know a little boy who has nothing to eat or wear, how could we be a "light" to him? We might bring him something to eat or give him a coat, and we will be a "light" to him.

Now watch. See this little candle. It is a little light, just as you should be little "lights." It throws out its rays in every direction. If the room were dark the candle's rays would be thrown out much further. The candle receives its burning power from the oxygen in the atmosphere which surrounds it but which you cannot see. Suppose there were no oxygen around the candle, what would happen to it? Shall we try to find out? Do you see this glass jar? We will put it over the candle. Watch the light. See what is happening? The candle has gone out. You see, there is no oxygen in the glass, which it needs in order to be a light.

As the candle needs the oxygen to give a good light, so we need God to be good "lights" in this world. If we try to be a "light" without God, we will be like the candle without oxygen; we will go out, we would not be "lights" at all.

So do not forget, "the Light of the world is Jesus," and that we, too, can be "lights." Jesus said, "Ye are the light of the world."

55

USING GOD'S GIFTS

Materials:

A quart milk bottle.
One marble.

Demonstration:

Place the marble in the milk bottle. The problem is how to keep the marble from falling out of the bottle when it is held with the mouth down and uncorked. Hold the bottle by the bottom, with the mouth upward. Move your hand in small circles fast enough to give the marble in the bottle a circular motion. As you continue the circular motion, gradually turn the bottle over. Centrifugal force will keep the marble going in a circle, pressed to the sides of the bottle just below the neck. As soon as you stop the circular motion the marble will fall out.

Story:

Let us say that this bottle is some person. Or let us say that it is you. And we will say that this marble is a talent. What is a talent? A talent is some gift that God has given you. By that I mean that God has given you something that you can do very well.

Perhaps God has given you a good voice, so that you can sing very well. You can sing better than most of the other boys and girls. You can sing so well that people like to hear you. That you can sing so well is a talent; it is a special gift which God has given to you. This bottle we said is you, and this marble is

your talent to sing. (Place marble in bottle.) As this
marble is in the bottle, so the talent to sing is in you.
But if I should turn the bottle upside down the marble
would fall out and be lost. How can I turn the bottle
upside down without losing the marble? You should
not lose your talent to sing, because God has given it
to you. Now let us see if I can turn the bottle upside
down without losing the marble. (Demonstrate.) I
am not losing the marble. If, however, I do not keep
the marble moving, even for only a second, I will lose
it. (Demonstrate.) So it is with you. You can
sing, but if you stop singing and do not use your voice
you will lose the talent God has given you.

God has given all of you some talent, something that
you can do very well. Some of you can stand up
before others and speak well. That is a talent. But if
you stop speaking before people you will lose this
talent. Remember that when I stop the marble I
lose it. Some of you can write well, others are good
in arithmetic, and still others can spell well. These are
talents. But be certain to keep your talents of writing,
working arithmetic, and spelling in motion. Keep on
doing these things. " Practice makes perfect." If you
stop you will lose these talents, just as I lose the marble
when I stop the motion.

If you keep a bird in a cage long enough, after a
while he will lose the ability to fly. If he does not
use his wings he will forget how to use them. Dr.
Aggrey of Africa told about a young eagle which a man
had found. The eagle is a very large bird, but this
one was very young and small. The man took the
young eagle home and put it in the yard with the
chickens. Five years later a visitor saw the eagle
among the chickens and said, " That bird is an eagle

and not a chicken." "Yes," said the owner, "but I have trained it to be a chicken; it is no longer an eagle." "No," said the other man, "it is still an eagle; it has the heart of an eagle, and I can make it fly high up to heaven." "No," said the owner, "it is now a chicken, and will never fly."

The visitor took the eagle in his hand and said, "Eagle, you are an eagle, you belong to the sky, not to this earth; stretch forth your wings and fly." The eagle only looked down, and seeing the chickens eating their food, it jumped down among them. The owner said, "I told you that it was a chicken." "No," said the other man, "it is an eagle. Give it another chance tomorrow." The next day the visitor tried again to induce the eagle to fly, but it would not. But the third day he took the eagle to the top of a hill just at the time when the sun was rising, and he said, "Eagle, you are an eagle; you belong to the sky, not to this earth; stretch out your wings and fly." But the eagle only looked around and would not fly. Then the man made the eagle look straight into the sun. Suddenly it stretched its large wings, and flapped them, and it flew higher and higher, right toward the sun, until it disappeared in the sky.

God has given the eagle a talent, something it can do very well. Its talent is flying. It can fly all day without tiring. But when this eagle was put into the chicken yard and did not use its wings, it almost lost its talent.

The eagle looked up into the sun, and when it saw the sun, it wanted to fly again. Too long it had been looking down and scratching in the dirt and dust of the chicken yard. God has made us to look up to Him, and not to look down at the dirt and dust. To look up to God is something we all can do. This is a special talent or gift God has given us. But when we stop looking to God we forget how to do it. The greatest talent God has given us is prayer. But if we do not pray we will lose this talent. The best way to keep God's gifts is to use them. Any talent that we do not use or keep in motion we will lose. Remember that when the marble was not kept in motion I lost it. (Demonstrate once more.)

Date Due